H. W. Carless (Henry William Carless) Davis

Balliol college

H. W. Carless (Henry William Carless) Davis

Balliol college

ISBN/EAN: 9783743309197

Manufactured in Europe, USA, Canada, Australia, Japa

Cover: Foto ©ninafisch / pixelio.de

Manufactured and distributed by brebook publishing software (www.brebook.com)

H. W. Carless (Henry William Carless) Davis

Balliol college

VIEW BY LOGGAN (1675)

University of Oxford

COLLEGE HISTORIES

BALLIOL COLLEGE

BY

H. W. CARLESS DAVIS, M.A.

FELLOW OF ALL SOULS COLLEGE,
SOMETIME SCHOLAR OF BALLIOL.

LONDON
F. E. ROBINSON AND CO.
20 GREAT RUSSELL STREET, BLOOMSBURY
1899

Printed by BALLANTYNE, HANSON & CO.
At the Ballantyne Press

PREFACE

An apology and an explanation may not be amiss from one who presents "a thrice-told tale" in yet another form. To the shade of Dr. Henry Savage my excuse is, that *Balliofergus* has been out of print for two centuries, in which space of time a good deal has happened to the society over which he presided. The Baroness de Paravicini and Mr. R. L. Poole, to both of whom I take this opportunity of expressing my indebtedness, will, I trust, pardon me for attempting to elucidate those parts of the College history on which their inclinations or their publishers forbade them to write at length.

My grateful thanks are due to the Master and Fellows of Balliol, first in their collective capacity, for allowing me a complete freedom of access to their records, and secondly as individuals, for the great kindness which they have shown on many occasions in answering a number of very tedious questions.

A list of the chief authorities, manuscript and printed,

which have been consulted in writing these pages will be found in an Appendix at the end of the volume.

In writing the last chapter of the book I have been much assisted by the criticisms and suggestions of Mr. Evelyn Abbott. The information contained in Appendix III. was kindly communicated by Mr. A. L. Smith. Throughout I am infinitely indebted to the suggestions of Mr. C. H. Firth, and of my colleague Mr. C. G. Robertson.

ALL SOULS, *August* 1, 1899.

CONTENTS

CHAP.		PAGE
I.	THE FOUNDATION OF BALLIOL	1
II.	SOMERVYLE'S STATUTES AND THE INTRODUCTION OF GRADUATE FELLOWS	22
III.	THE RENAISSANCE AND THE OLD LIBRARY	41
IV.	BISHOP FOX'S STATUTES	62
V.	THE OLD CHAPEL AND THE REFORMATION	76
VI.	JESUIT AND PURITAN, 1559–1603	95
VII.	PURITAN AND ANGLICAN—BLUNDELL'S TRUST	112
VIII.	THE CIVIL WAR AND COMMONWEALTH	130
IX.	THE RESTORATION AND THE REVOLUTION	148
X.	BALLIOL IN THE EIGHTEENTH CENTURY	168
XI.	MODERN BALLIOL	193
	APPENDICES	224
	INDEX	233

ILLUSTRATIONS

VIEW BY LOGGAN (1675)	*Frontispiece*	
FRONT OF THE COLLEGE, FROM BROAD STREET	*Facing page*	8
THE FELLOWS' GARDEN	,,	18
THE OLD LIBRARY	,,	46
FRONT QUADRANGLE, LOOKING WEST	,,	64
BACK GATE AND MARTYRS' MEMORIAL	,,	88
FISHER'S BUILDINGS	,,	170
THE NEW HALL	,,	220

CHAPTER I

THE FOUNDATION OF BALLIOL

Principals:* Walter of Fotheringhay, 1282; Hugh of Warkenby, 1296; Stephen of Cornwall, 1303; Richard of Chickwell, 1309.

AMONG European universities those of England stand alone to-day in their adhesion to the collegiate system. Others have resented the existence of these subsidiary institutions as soon as they began to show the slightest trace of individual character and independent volition. Oxford and Cambridge, at first spontaneously, then under the pressure of the royal prerogative, welcomed the College as a valuable servant. The motives for this friendly attitude have varied from age to age. At their inception Colleges were regarded as a means of attracting more students to the University; later on as useful instruments for enforcing discipline and religious conformity; to-day as centres of social life and as tutorial organisations. But of such jealousies as existed in other universities, between the central governing bodies and the authorities of the Colleges there established, there are few traces in the history of Oxford and Cambridge.

* Until the fifteenth century it is out of the question to give the exact date of each election, or to be certain that the list is complete. Here and in the next chapter we give the date at which each Principal or Master is first mentioned.

Friction of a kind there has always been, but the friction has arisen on questions of detail.

Yet the collegiate system, congenial as it has proved to the English mind, can hardly be claimed as an English invention, though true it is that the first of such societies, that of the Hôtel Dieu in Paris was endowed by an English pilgrim (1180). His experiment attracted some notice; it was imitated and improved upon by several pious founders; but for more than half a century these imitations and improvements were made in Paris alone. Paris tried the new institution in most of its possible forms before other universities were fired to emulation.

A College is essentially a society of students, united together by the possession of exclusive privileges and participation in endowments, of whom most live under one common roof, and all are subject to a common discipline, upheld by resident officials. Within these limits the College may be turned to very various purposes. It may be no more than an endowed hostel, in which all the inmates stand on the same footing, in which the government is democratic. Such Colleges are only indirectly connected with educational purposes. They do not teach, but they give poor students an opportunity of residing in a place where they may be taught. This is the first and simplest type of a College, the type represented by the Hôtel Dieu. More highly developed types soon made their appearance. There was, for example, the seminary founded by some corporate body, such as a monastery, to promote the diffusion of knowledge among the members of that body. In Oxford the College of the monks of Durham, and the

Hall founded by the Benedictines of St. Peter at Gloucester are the most remarkable instances of such seminaries. Or, again, the college might be designed to propagate a peculiar set of principles among those who took the University on the way to a professional life. This was the character of such Colleges as the Mendicant Orders founded in Paris, and would have liked to found in Oxford. Other founders, in a less sectarian spirit, aimed merely at encouraging the pursuit of learning and philosophy in one or more of their numerous branches and subdivisions. Of this kind was the College of the Sorbonne, which St. Louis of France assisted his chaplain, Brother Robert, to found in the year 1257; in Oxford, Merton, New College and All Souls were founded with a similar intention. Finally, the College may aim at becoming a place of general education for the young, and in particular for those who, without assistance, would miss the opportunity of studying the liberal sciences. This ideal, to which, with very few exceptions, all existing Colleges have pledged themselves, is first to be found in the Parisian Collège d'Harcourt which, not content with aiding the needy, expressly provided for the reception of those who could pay for the advantages conferred.

The College which is the subject of the following pages conformed, in its original shape, to the earliest and simplest of the types above described. So far as we know, it represents the first attempt to establish a body corporate of students within the larger corporation of the University to which they belonged; and the founders had neither the desire nor the requisite means to make the new institution in any way a rival of the

University. It disclaimed educational functions, it exercised only the most moderate control over its inmates.

At the close of the Barons' War (1266), when the University of Oxford retired for a time from the political feuds into which she had thrown herself with so much vigour, and settled down for a period of quiet development, her institutions were of the most rudimentary description. There was a Chancellor elected by the University and vested with exclusive rights of jurisdiction in all but the most important cases. There was a Congregation of Masters, which claimed and sometimes exercised the right of making statutes. There were also two Proctors, representing the northern and the southern "nations" respectively. But the powers and duties of these officials and of the legislative assembly of Masters were extremely uncertain. It was still possible for questions of the highest moment to be settled by a general mass-meeting of all the students, whether graduates or not.

In ordinary matters the students were left to govern themselves, and this privilege they used or abused to the utmost. But so little was a solitary life in lodgings congenial to their temper, that from a very early period they adopted the Parisian system of grouping themselves together in voluntary associations, of hiring a common abode, and of making customs for their own government. Usually, they elected from among their own number a Principal to administer these statutes, to disburse the common funds, and to represent them in all dealings with their landlord. At the time of which we are writing the power of the students to make their own by-laws and to elect their own Head was practically unlimited.

Halls of this kind might have remained for a long time the only rallying-point among the students but for the influence of the Church. She had learned the importance of the Universities in the intellectual controversies of the first half of the thirteenth century. She had recognised that mere intimidation would not suffice to quell the spirit of rationalism which now and again appeared in the teaching of the Schools. It was far better to turn the weapon of her enemies against themselves, to use the Universities as her recruiting ground, and to lose no opportunity of extending her influence among the students. For this purpose the friendship of institutions was more valuable than that of individuals. In the minds of ecclesiastics the idea rapidly gained ground that if students could be drawn into endowed foundations their conduct and their studies could be more rigidly supervised, their minds might be moulded to the type desired, and a strong claim upon their services might be established. The earliest Colleges were founded by individual benefactors, often by laymen; but everywhere we discern the guiding hand of the Church, and the underlying assumption that sooner or later the recipients of the founder's bounty will seek and obtain a position in the hierarchy.

Although not intended as a place of theological study, Balliol is a striking monument of this policy so silently and tenaciously pursued by the Church. The foundation of the College was commanded by a Bishop of Durham and directed by the Franciscan Order. The larger half of the credit belongs to the Grey Friars.

From the moment of their first landing in England they had realised the importance of Oxford as a centre of intellectual life. Their house in the parish of St. Benedict, outside the city wall, played from an early period a conspicuous part in the life of the University. They admitted under their roof lay scholars, often of noble rank. They borrowed teachers from the University, and afterwards repaid the loan with interest by producing some of the profoundest thinkers who contributed to shape the thought of mediæval Europe. The Oxford convent was at once a school for the Order and the centre of an important propaganda. But, since practice rather than theory had always been the aim of the Order, they were anxious not merely to capture the first intellects of the University, but also to obtain some measure of control over the undistinguished unambitious students who then as always formed the rank and file.

A natural sympathy for the weaker side led them to court with especial eagerness the friendship of the Northern "nation," whose ranks were recruited from Scotland and beyond the Trent. And in this charitable work they were assisted by their local connections. York was the centre of one of the most thriving Wardenries in the English province of the Order. We discern a steady influx of students from the north into the Oxford convent, and in many cases these students returned at the conclusion of their course to hold preferment in their native homes, or to act as the father-confessors of the great baronial houses, which almost in proportion as they emancipated themselves from the grip of the State fell under the less galling control of the Church. It was a most natural consequence that some part of the wealth possessed by these barons should ultimately be diverted to the uses of the Oxford Franciscans and to the charitable purposes which they had most at heart.

*Few families in the ranks of the northern nobility could claim to rank above the Balliols of Barnard Castle. In England they were the lords of thirty knights' fees; in Normandy they held the wide lands of Harcourt and Bailleul; and to these possessions John of Balliol, the chief of the house at the time of which we speak, had added by his marriage with the Lady Dervorguilla one half of the Scottish earldom of Galloway. In the district immediately surrounding Barnard Castle John of Balliol ruled with all the attributes of a petty sovereign, enjoying, in the language of feudal law, "the low, the middle and the high justice." But, great as he was, he found the Bishop-Palatine of Durham a sore thorn in his side. Their possessions marched together, and disputes as to boundaries inevitably arose, which would have been troublesome enough to the Balliols if their adversary had been a mere lay-baron without the adventitious assistance of spiritual authority and royal favour. The struggle was bound to be one-sided; more especially as Walter Chirkham, the holder of the see during the latter years of Henry III., was a worthy successor of the great Hugh Puiset. "Little in body, but great in mind," as his admiring biographer describes him, he never pardoned an insult or acquiesced in a

---

* The authorities upon which the following account is based are: *The Chronicle of Lanercost* (ed. Stevenson), p. 69; *The Chronicle of Melrose*, s.a. 1269; Surtees' *History of Durham*; with the comments of Mr. Maxwell Lyte and Mr. Poole.

defeat; and John of Balliol, after a brief period of arrogant triumph, was forced in a very literal sense to kiss the dust before the Bishop's feet.

Our story begins in the year 1255, when Walter Chirkham had laid some of the Balliol retainers under the ban of excommunication, for disseising him of lands which he claimed as the property of his See. The retort of Balliol was rough and ready. He laid an ambush for the Bishop, subjected him when captured to some indignities, and carried off a part of his retinue. The Bishop laid his complaint before the King, and obtained a writ condemning the outrage in the strongest language and demanding instant reparation. From loyalty or calculation the offender submitted, and the men of Durham were edified by the spectacle of this haughty baron prostrating himself in penitential garb before the doors of their Cathedral, while the Bishop applied the scourge with no gentle hand. The humiliation was no doubt endured with the better grace as Balliol retained possession, in part at least, of the disputed lands; in 1297 the claims of the see of Durham were still unsatisfied. Still the penance, so far as it went, was performed with a good grace. The Bishop demanded that it should be crowned by a substantial act of charity; and in obedience to the mandate John hired a house in the suburbs of Oxford, near the church of St. Mary Magdalen, and made it a hostel for the reception of sixteen poor scholars, to each of whom he made an allowance of eightpence a day. So far the chroniclers; and their witness is confirmed by the evidence of a royal writ,* dated June 1266, in which

---

* *Calendar of Scotch Documents* (ed. Bain), p. 476.

THE FOUNDATION OF BALLIOL.   9

Henry III. orders the Mayor and Bailiffs to advance out of the fee-farm which they owe to the Crown the sum of £20 to John of Balliol "for the use of the Scholars whom he maintains in the said town."

The house hired by John of Balliol stood in Horsemonger Street (the modern Broad Street), facing the moat and the city wall. It belonged to the University, and is called by antiquarians sometimes Old Balliol Hall and sometimes Sparrow Hall. On the west it was flanked by tenements belonging to St. Frideswide's which extended to the corner of the street; on the east by nine or ten small houses of which the most remote occupied the south-eastern corner of the modern front-quadrangle. Behind the houses lay a labyrinth of small gardens, groves of trees, and footwalks; the rectangular area now covered by the College buildings was partitioned between a number of owners. The surroundings of the original scholars of Balliol were squalid enough, and their lodgings were no more commodious than might have been expected from the neighbourhood. They can hardly have attracted much attention by their arrival; for there was little to distinguish Balliol Hall from those established by voluntary enterprise. There were no statutes; the scholars framed their own customs and elected their own Principal. They were not a legal corporation for they had no common seal* and no property. Their weekly dole was paid to them by the hands of John of

---

* The first Common Seal of the College represented the Virgin seated with the Child in her arms, surrounded by St. Catharine and other saints. No example of it is now to be found in the Archives (*Balliofergus*, p. 81). The second, in use till 30 Eliz., is figured in Ingram, *Memorials of Oxford* (*Balliol*, p. 1).

Balliol's agents; they had no guarantee for its continuance. Their benefactor did indeed design to make a permanent provision for them; but he was cut off in the year 1269, and for more than a decade after that event the newly formed society stood in imminent danger of dissolution. Until 1284 there was neither a charter nor an endowment. Meanwhile Walter of Merton had succeeded in his design of establishing a College on the opposite side of the city; the form of Merton College may be regarded as definitely fixed by the year 1274; and it is therefore idle to claim priority for Balliol. The society of the scholars of Balliol existed from at least the year 1266; and many of the customs and traditions formed in it were grafted upon the later foundation of 1284. But the existence of the College as a true corporate body undoubtedly dates from the latter year.

The credit of completing what John of Balliol had begun belongs to his wife, the Lady Dervorguilla of Galloway. Great indeed would have been the surprise of that stout old obscurantist her husband to learn that he and she would be chiefly known to posterity as the benefactors of a few poor scholars. In his eyes it would be of far greater moment that he had once held the Regency of Scotland, and that he had been foremost in opposition to the usurper Montfort. With his wife it was different. The scholars of Balliol occupied a large place in her thoughts; she spent her money and her energies in their service; she treated them as trusted friends. There is just cause to complain of the neglect with which she has been repaid. If there is any trust to be placed in chroniclers she was a lady of more than passable comeliness; but the one portrait of her which is to be found in Balliol is not only apocryphal but what is worse, a libel on the female sex. It is a slight consolation to be assured by Hearne that the original was the leading Oxford beauty of his day. We can only plead in exculpation that our own age, though often taunted with unseemly neglect of tradition, has sinned less deeply than the sixteenth and seventeenth centuries. In those days the College came near to losing the very name of the founders, for it was commonly known to its neighbours as "Bayly Hall"; and though Balliol men never sank to this degree of ignorance, they were accustomed to claim as their founder King Edward Balliol, whose only connection with the foundation of his grandparents lies in the fact that he confirmed grants which it was out of his power to annul.

*Though Dervorguilla ruled by hereditary right over one of the most uncouth and lawless districts in southern Scotland, she had been educated in England at the court of her grandfather David, Earl of Huntingdon, and there was little enough of the fierce Galwegian in her composition. Of her married life we know nothing, but her widowhood was passed in the company of the religious, and her chief occupation seems to have been the planning of good works which should perpetuate her husband's memory. In Galloway she built Sweetheart Abbey as a resting-place for the heart of John of Balliol. In Oxford she aimed at securing the welfare

---

* The following account is chiefly based upon the documents in the Archives and the calendars of Mr. Riley and Mr. Parker (the latter MS.).

of his scholars. She persuaded his executors to engage that of the sums disbursed in charity from the dead man's estate, some part should go to Balliol Hall; and pending the fulfilment of these promises she continued the usual allowances from her own purse.

Little could be done till the Hall had received a constitution. At the first opportunity she addressed a code of Statutes, in the form of a letter, to the agents (*Procuratores*) by whom the Balliol dole had been hitherto distributed. Their names were William de Menyl and Brother Hugh of Hartlepool; the former was a Master of Arts in the University, the latter a Franciscan friar residing in the Oxford convent. The mention of this friar is our first intimation of the close bond which seems to have existed from the first between Balliol Hall and the community in St. Benedict's parish. An explanation of this bond has been suggested above. So close was it that already in 1284 the Bishop of Lincoln speaks of many members of the House who have devoted themselves to the religious life.* Until the Statutes of Bishop Fox were promulgated (1507) one of the Visitors of the College was always a Franciscan.

The Statutes which the Procurators were instructed to put in force do not claim to be exhaustive. They assume that the Hall is already governed by customary rules, and leave the scholars to settle many questions for themselves. In all probability some parts of them are nothing more than a formal statement of usages which had prevailed from the beginning.† But they

* *Linc. Reg.* f. 74 *b*. Quoted by Mr. Rashdall.
† *E.g.*, the authority of the Principal is to be "*secundum statuta consuetudines inter ipsos usitata et approbata*" (*Statutes*, p. 1).

are the first historical document by which any light is thrown upon the social life of the Hall, and it would be rash to aim at distinguishing what is new in them from what is old.

The Foundress does not mention the number of the scholars who are to be supported by her bounty; only from documents of a later date do we discover that custom had already fixed it at sixteen. She does not name the time for which the scholars may continue to receive their allowances; but we know that, according to the ruling of the Visitors, a generation after her death, the scholars lost their places on the Foundation when they became Masters of Arts, and that they were not allowed to delay this consummation by neglecting the course in Arts for the lectures of other Faculties. The only subjects with which the Statutes deal in any detail are, the authority of the Procurators, the office of the Principal, and the daily life of the scholars. The scholars were to attend divine service on Sundays and Feast Days, and every year to celebrate three solemn masses for the souls of the co-founders. On ordinary days they should attend the schools, and pursue their studies according to the statutes of the University. Within the house their conversation must be in the Latin language; and once a week all were to meet together and hold a disputation on a subject announced by the Principal. Two meals, breakfast and supper, were to be provided at the common table, to the maintenance of which the allowances or commons were principally devoted. If in any one week the cost of the common table should exceed the aggregate of allowances, then the scholars were to be assessed in proportion to their means for the payment of the deficit; those in straitened circumstances were not to be called upon for more than one penny in any week. In the House there was always to be one "poor scholar" maintained upon the crumbs of the common table. The Principal was elected by the scholars from among themselves, and was to be obeyed "according to the Statutes and customs used and approved." His election was only valid when confirmed by the Procurators, and, as the administration of all the corporate property was vested in the hands of these last, his chief duty was that of enforcing discipline within the House. He presided at table and at the disputations; he could suspend those who disregarded his commands from the society of the common table; such offenders were to be served separately and after all the rest. But a sentence of expulsion could only be pronounced by the Procurators. The latter, besides managing the funds and paying the allowances, were charged to hear all complaints and to tax the scholars for their contributions to the common table. They were to be obeyed in all matters that concerned the order and well-being of the House.

Nothing is said in these statutes about the College buildings. The students were still lodged in their hired house, from which Dervorguilla designed to remove them at the earliest opportunity. But from the statutes it is obvious that the dining-hall was the focus of social life. Here the table would be spread, and here the disputations would be held. Here too in all probability the students would pursue their private reading under the eye of the Principal, since there is no mention of a library until a much later period. For

THE FOUNDATION OF BALLIOL

divine service the scholars resorted, even after their removal to a more spacious abode, to the parish church of St. Mary Magdalen. The north aisle was repaired by the Lady Dervorguilla and fitted up as an oratory for her scholars. For this reason it was known long afterwards as St. Catharine's chapel; already the scholars had adopted as their patroness the virgin-martyr of Alexandria.

The next step taken by the Foundress was to grant a fitting endowment. Towards the end of the year 1283 or at the beginning of 1284, she purchased, with the help of her husband's executors, certain lands and rents in Stamfordham and Howgh, in the county of Northumberland. These she assigned to the Principal and scholars "to have and to hold to them and to their successors, dwelling according to the Statutes in Oxford or wheresoever else that University of Oxford shall happen to be transferred." The migration to Northampton of 1262-4 was still fresh in the minds of the scholars, and it was even yet far from certain that Oxford would be the permanent abode of the University. But although Dervorguilla provided for the possibility of a removal she went on to make it difficult by giving to her scholars a house of their own in Oxford. In 1284 she purchased a block of three tenements lying a little to the east of Old Balliol Hall, converted them into a single house suitable for the needs of a student community, and removed the scholars thither. New Balliol Hall, or Mary Hall, as it was variously called, stood on the south-west side of the present front quadrangle. It faced the street and was surrounded on three sides by garden ground of which a part belonged to it.

In making these arrangements Dervorguilla was guided by a Franciscan, Richard of Slikeburne. Tradition states that he was her confessor, but there is little to support this conjecture in the documents from which our knowledge of him is derived. The first of these is a letter addressed to him by Dervorguilla and dated 1284.* After a preface in which she states that at the instance of many men of great consideration, both religious and secular, she has resolved to continue the almsgiving of her husband, she makes the request that he will be her attorney in the business of the said scholars, and empowers him to appoint what Procurators he will for the management of the endowment. The name of Slikeburne denotes that the friar was a native of Durham, and there are certain expressions in the letter which imply a previous acquaintanceship between himself and Dervorguilla. She calls him her "dearly beloved brother in Christ" and speaks of "our complete confidence in your discretion and devotion." Two more documents in the archives show that Slikeburne continued to exercise his trust for several years. In 1285 he persuaded the executors of John of Balliol to grant the sum of £100 to the scholars, and in 1287 we find him confirming a further donation of all the debts which were due to John of Balliol at the time of his death. These amounted to more than £900, and, could they have been collected in full, would have more than doubled the endowment. But some of them were of twenty or thirty years' standing, and although the first Principal of the Hall pursued the debtors with great energy it

* Literally transcribed by the Baroness de Paravicini, *Early History*, &c., p. 71.

THE FOUNDATION OF BALLIOL.

does not appear that any considerable portion of the sums due was ever recovered.

The first Principal elected under the Statutes was a certain Walter of Fotheringhay. A native of the place in which Dervorguilla had spent her early years and where she frequently resided during her widowhood, he appears to have enjoyed an unusual measure of her confidence, and was one of the executors whom she appointed under her will.* The first mention of him occurs in deeds of the years 1283–4. He was ultimately promoted to a prebend at Lincoln, doubtless through the favour of the Bishop, Oliver Sutton. The Foundress had been careful to secure for her Scholars the protection of their diocesan, as well as that of the Chancellor of the University. The new Statutes were confirmed by Bishop Sutton in the year 1284, and his successors appear to have construed the confirmation as implying a right on their part to visit the College when they pleased.

Dervorguilla's death occurred in the year 1289. She left by her will a legacy of £100 to the Principal and Scholars; but in spite of the fact that the Principal himself was one of the executors, considerable difficulty was experienced in bringing the Balliol family to discharge the obligation. A part of the sum remained unpaid till the year 1330; the College sued the son of their benefactress in the Chancery without much effect; it was from her grandson Edward Balliol that they at length obtained satisfaction. Fortunately their financial position was sound, and they do not appear to have suffered materially from this delay. For some years

* *Cal. Rot. Pat.* 1281–1292, p. 413.

after the death of Dervorguilla they continued to add to their landed property, partly through purchases, partly through gifts from former members of the House. By the year 1310 the whole of the site of the front quadrangle had passed into their hands. On the west this site was enclosed by Old Balliol Hall, which still belonged to the University; on the north their boundary was a line drawn from the east end of the parish church to the land of the monks of Durham, a part of which is marked to-day by the walk running east and west under the north wall of the Fellows' Garden. It is unlikely that they appropriated the whole of this land for their own uses. Small as it was, Balliol Hall offered accommodation enough for sixteen poor scholars. The newly acquired tenements would for the most part be treated as an investment and let, to the highest bidder. In other parts of the city the College acquired Hert Hall and St. Hugh's Hall (1290), Chimers Hall (1311), land lying in Merton Street between Lomb Hall and St. Albans' Hall (1316), and several houses in School Street (1310-1317). The last-named thoroughfare ran almost in a straight line from the west end of the University Church past Brasenose Hall and as far as the city-wall. Near the top of the street, on the left-hand side, Balliol held a block of four tenements, which were let at a rent to disputants, and commonly known as the Balliol Schools. The land on which they stood is now occupied by a part of the Divinity Schools and the University still pays the College a quit-rent on this account.

* The most important of the bequests made to the

* For Burnel's donation *cf.* Rashdall, vol. ii. p. 759. *Balliofergus*, p. 27.

From a Photograph by the] THE FELLOWS' GARDEN. *[Oxford Camera Club*

THE FOUNDATION OF BALLIOL

College at this time has a curious history. Oxford was the seat of a large Jewish colony, whose ghetto extended along the east side of St. Aldates, from the corner opposite Carfax to the site of Tom Gate. The whole of this property fell in to the King when he expelled the Jews from England in the year 1289; and amongst the grants which he made from the spoil he gave to William Burnel, Archdeacon of Wells, the Synagogue and nine houses adjacent to it, of which one was built over the South Gate. William Burnel and his brother, the King's minister, had the intention of founding on this site a college of their own, and for three years a community of scholars was maintained there. But on the death of Robert Burnel the scheme was abandoned; in 1305 William bequeathed the Synagogue and the tenements composing Burnel's Inn to Balliol College. Nine years elapsed before the Principal and Scholars could make good their claim to the legacy; for Hugh le Despenser, acting in the name of the Crown, took possession of the houses, on the ground that Burnel had no right to leave this kind of property by will. Ultimately, however, the judges decided that houses in Oxford were devisable according to the customs of the city; and in 1314, while Edward II. was absent in the north, the bequest was confirmed by Margaret the Queen Dowager, whose writ with her seal appended is still to be seen in the archives.

The College has long since parted with the houses in School Street, with Hert Hall, and with Burnel's Inn. But in 1294 it purchased a London property of which it still retains the nominal ownership.* This comprises

* The St. Lawrence Jewry tenements were let in the last century

the advowson of St. Lawrence Jewry, a soke of land, and some houses in the same parish. They gave for it the sum of one hundred marks to Hugh of Vienne, which seemingly was something less than the full market value; for the name of Hugh of Vienne was inscribed upon the list of benefactors, and until the Elizabethan reformation he was regularly remembered in the prayers of the College.

With the commencement of the fourteenth century the first chapter in the College history comes to an end, for immediately afterwards began a series of disputes which resulted in sweeping alterations of the original constitution. Balliol, as Dervorguilla had left it, was a society composed entirely of undergraduates. Though closely connected with a religious Order, it was not intended to be a place of theological studies, and the Scholars were to depart as soon as they had completed the elementary course in Arts. The House was emphatically a poor one; food and lodging of a moderate quality were the only advantages to be expected from a scholarship. Hence the ties which bound the Scholars to the House were slight, and although a residence of six or seven years was always possible, they would have every inducement to look about them for some other home. A few years would be sufficient to work a complete change in the character of the persons composing the Society, and we are not surprised to find that customs also changed with great rapidity. There was the less stability since the Scholars had not the right of co-opting to vacant places. This was vested in the Pro-

to the City of London at a fixed corn-rent, their removal being needed for municipal improvements.

curators, who were strangers to the House, and whose choice of candidates was guided entirely by their own tastes and prejudices. Perhaps the chances of a corrupt election were diminished by this arrangement, but, on the other hand, it prevented the perpetuation of a normal type of Scholar, and left the House a fortuitous concourse of individuals. The maintenance of permanent traditions and the growth of *esprit de corps* were out of the question until two important changes in the constitution should be effected. It was necessary, in the first place, to make the lot of the ordinary Scholar more attractive, that he might be induced to prolong his term of residence; and secondly, to provide for the introduction of a graduate element which, by example and authority, might uphold the ancient usages. The benefactions and the statutes by which this conservative reform was wrought will be the subject of our second chapter.

CHAPTER II

SOMERVILLE'S STATUTES AND THE INTRODUCTION OF GRADUATE FELLOWS

Principals: Thomas of Waldeby, 1321; Henry of Seton, 1323; Nicholas of Luceby, 1327; John Poclynton, 1332.
Masters: Hugh Corbrygge, 1340; Robert of Derby, 1356; John Wyclif, 1360; John Hugate, 1366; Thomas Tyrwhit, 1371; Hamond Haskman, 1397.

THE fourteenth century found Oxford already committed to the collegiate system. If we may be allowed to count University, which was then, and remained for some years, in a chrysalis stage, a little superior to the ordinary Hall and a good deal inferior to the full-blown College, there were in the year 1300 three Colleges already in existence, and about the same number of Halls had been endowed by various monastic houses. The next hundred years saw the foundation of Exeter (1314), Oriel (1324), Queen's (1341), and New College (1379). By 1400, although it was probably still a numerical minority of the students who were housed within the walls of such foundations, the annals of the University make frequent allusions to certain Colleges, and it is plain that their corporate sympathies and tenets were forces to be reckoned with in all academical controversies. The men of Merton and Queen's were, for example, the life and soul of Wyclif's party; and in the far older quarrel of North and South these and the other Colleges lost no time in ranging themselves on one side or the other.

The Colleges, however, which thrust themselves upon the notice of historians were few in number. Balliol, the most ancient House of all, is rarely mentioned, and never as a home of violent partisans. It is true that Richard of Armagh and John Wyclif were trained within her walls, but the theories for which they became famous do not appear to have been framed before they had migrated, the one to Durham College, the other to Queen's, and they never found conspicuous supporters in Balliol. It is true also that Balliol possessed for many years a distinctively Northern character which would naturally have exposed her sons to attack from the Southern faction; but even in this mock-serious feud she studied moderation. Those who believe in the influence of geography upon history may, perhaps, be inclined to maintain that this immunity from strife was due to the suburban position of Balliol, and that if the College had been situated anywhere between Carfax and the University Church there would have been a very different story to tell. There are other and perhaps more adequate explanations of the facts, or shall we say of the absence of facts? The poverty of the Balliol Scholars appears to have been quite exceptional, and this would cut away the desire and the possibility of associating with the members of other Colleges; the more so as their academic standing was the lowest possible. If there had been many Masters of Arts in the

College, their votes would have given her a certain importance. But the Balliol men could only assist an ally with nature's weapons, and even in the frays of the streets their numbers were so small as to leave them inconsiderable. Then, again, their poverty made them cautious and preoccupied. Their only prospect of advancement lay in the favour of the Church, and this could be secured with more certainty by a diligent attention to Priscian and Aristotle than by a hardy plunge into polemics. Whatever time could be spared from lectures and disputations they seem to have employed in canvassing potential benefactors, and in wrangling with the Procurators upon whom they depended for their supplies. Their allowances and their privileges were of far more moment to them than the iniquities of the Friars or the doctrine of Dominion.

The Procurators were always, until their abolition by Bishop Fox, a thorn in the side of the College. For this they were not altogether to blame. After the manner of their kind they were intensely anxious that the wishes of the Founder should be respected; and it was only natural that they should overrule the considerations of expediency which the Scholars urged in favour of laxer rules. It was equally natural that where a dispute arose as to the exact sense of the Statutes they should prefer their own interpretation. On the other hand, we cannot be surprised that the Scholars chafed against the unsympathetic rulings of an external authority, when they fancied that their future prospects were in jeopardy. The Statutes of Dervorguilla afforded many opportunities of dispute, and we are not surprised to find that in 1325 the Scholars and their Visitors fell

out over the question of studies. The course for the
degree of Master in Arts was not particularly severe,
though the list of books prescribed was formidable. A
very moderate degree of proficiency enabled the student
to obtain the required certificate from those graduates
with whom he was acquainted, and such a certificate was
the only test imposed by the University. There was
therefore nothing to hinder the ambitious from pushing
forward with the more advanced subjects of Theology
and Law, while they were still technically unqualified
for the courses of these faculties. There was no clause
in Dervorguilla's Statutes which expressly prohibited her
Scholars from making this use of their spare time. But
to the Procurators it seemed that those who followed
these bypaths were defrauding the foundation and the
candidates who were waiting for a vacancy to occur.
The Scholar should allow nothing to divert him from
his main business of obtaining the Master's degree at
the earliest opportunity. If he wished to proceed
further he might then betake himself to some other
College, where there was provision made for graduates.
This was the answer made to an appeal of the Principal
and Scholars in 1325, after a solemn hearing in the
College Hall. Though a severe blow to the appellants,
the decision seems to have been strictly in accordance
with the customs of the House, for it was confirmed by
several former Scholars who were present at the proceedings, and in particular by Richard of Armagh, who
thus, for once in his life, found himself of the same
opinion as a Friar. Richard of Armagh was already a
person of some importance in the University. He
seems, when by graduation he had become disqualified

for the further tenure of a Balliol scholarship, to have found an asylum among the monks of Durham College. In 1333 he became either Chancellor or Vice-Chancellor of the University, and thus started on that successful career which culminated in his appointment to the Archbishopric of Armagh (1347). While acquiescing in the decision of the Procurators on the present occasion, he took to heart the necessities of his old College. In the endowments by which these necessities were subsequently relieved his influence can be clearly traced.

Some years, however, were to elapse before his good intentions could be realised. Meanwhile, the Scholars continued as before to leave the College immediately upon taking their degree. Many remained in Oxford; some, we are told, after fruitless endeavours to obtain a benefice, drifted into mechanical employments, and resigned themselves to the loss of those advantages which they had expected to gain by their education. A few migrated to foreign Universities. A strange accident has preserved the history of Stephen de Cornubia, who was one of these adventurers. There is in the College Library a manuscript of Galen which was once in his possession. A note on the fly-leaf relates that he went to Paris and there took his degree as Doctor of Medicine. He gave the book to a friend who afterwards became a Fellow of Peterhouse, Cambridge; ultimately it passed into the hands of a Fellow of Balliol, who presented it to the College Library.

The sole event of the years immediately following 1325 was the erection of the first College Chapel. Since the year 1293 the Scholars had rejoiced in the possession of a private Oratory, and a Chaplain had been provided in 1310 by the liberality of Hugh de Warkenby and William de Gotham. But this Oratory was merely an ordinary room fitted up for the purpose, and no ecclesiastical Sacrament might be celebrated there. On all festivals, and whenever they wished to say a Mass in memory of their Founders, the Scholars were still bound to resort to their parish Church. In 1327 they set about building a real Chapel, in which all divine services might be performed. The one record of the fact is a deed in the archives recording the liberal assistance which they received from Nicholas Quappelad, Abbot of Reading. Besides the sum of £20, which he had been commissioned to expend for the health of the soul of Adam Poleter, a burgess of Reading, the Abbot gave on his own part ten marks of silver, a quantity of laths and timber, and a glass window worth more than £10. The building to which these gifts were made remained in use as a Chapel until 1529, and is conjecturally identified with the dining-room of the Master's House. The oriel window of this room is one of the most salient features of the front quadrangle, and, although we know it to have been rebuilt in the fifteenth century at the cost of George Nevill, whose arms it bears, there is reason to believe that his architect preserved the original design. The room has a lofty roof and faces due east. Until 1869 the bay of the oriel window was filled by a raised daïs which may well have marked the position of the altar; the entrance to the room is by folding doors at the west end.

Meanwhile the College and its needs had attracted the attention of Richard Bury, Bishop of Durham. It was natural that the successor of Walter Chirkham should take some interest in Balliol; but Richard Bury was probably stimulated by the exhortations of Richard of Armagh, who was his friend and chaplain. The College could hardly have found a more useful patron than this Mæcenas of the North. The interest which Richard Bury took in scholarship is attested by the magnificent collection of manuscripts which he gave to Durham College, and by the treatise *Philobiblon* which he wrote to explain the way in which books should be used, and the precautions to be taken for their preservation.* His palace was a school for all the noble youth of his diocese, and the influence which he thus acquired with their families was employed in the service of learning. His own profusion left him without the means to become a benefactor in his own person. But he discovered two barons who were willing to spend some money on charitable purposes, and persuaded them to select Balliol as the object of their bounty.

The first of the new endowments came, in the year 1340, from a certain Sir William Felton. There were two persons of this name alive in 1340. The younger and more famous of them figures in the pages of Froissart as seneschal of Poitou and the hero of doughty deeds which made him the wonder of his age; but it is more natural to suppose that the gift now in question came from his father, the lord of the constabulary of Medomsley in the palatinate of Durham. The gift took the form of a benefice. Subject to the consent of

* Wood states that in the reign of Edward VI. part of the Bishop's library came into the possession of Balliol. But this is a mere conjecture. None of the Balliol MSS. can be traced to this source, and there is no other evidence to show what became of the Durham books.

the King and the Pope, Felton impropriated to the use of the Master and Scholars of Balliol the tithes and glebe of Abboldesley in the earldom of Huntingdon. The revenues accruing therefrom were to be expended in relieving the most crying needs of the Scholars. A part of them was to raise the weekly allowances from eightpence to twelvepence; with another part books and clothes were to be purchased. Out of the surplus the allowances of those who had graduated were to be continued, until they should obtain for themselves a competent ecclesiastical benefice. The total value of the revenues of Abboldesley was officially estimated at something less than £40 per annum.

Some years, however, elapsed before the Scholars felt the benefit of the augmentation. The King gave his licence in April 1340; that of the Pope was not obtained till 1343.* Even after this the Scholars had to wait until the existing Rector should vacate the benefice, and this did not occur until 1361. In that year the Scholars, according to the directions of the Pope, made an agreement with the Bishop of Lincoln for the maintenance of a Vicar. The Bishop drove a hard bargain. All the tithes and sixty acres of the glebe were reserved for the Vicar; the College furthermore undertook to build him a parsonage, to pay him an annual pension of five shillings, and to keep the chancel of the Church in repair; little of the £40 a year can have remained when these requirements were satisfied.† After all the preliminaries had been duly transacted, the Master of the

---

* *Cal. Papal Registers. Petitions* i. p. 16. Paravicini, p. 168.

† The glebe which the College holds in Abboldesley is now about 139 acres in extent.

College took possession in the prescribed form. He rang the bells of the Church, touched the plate upon the altar, and took possession of the rector's house. These trivial details become interesting when we find that the Master in question was John Wyclif. He entered the House about the time when Felton's grant was made, and he kept up his residence just long enough to see the grant made good.

Long before they touched the Felton benefaction the Principal and Scholars had carried out a part of the changes which it was intended to further. They were enabled to do so through the liberality of Sir Philip Somervyle, who came to their aid in the same year as Felton, but a few months later. The Somervyles were a Norman family, tracing their descent from one of the Conqueror's barons. Wichnor, the head of their barony, was in the county of Stafford, but from a very early date they had formed connections and acquired estates in the far north. A younger branch of the family migrated to Scotland in 1164, founded the barony of Linton, and fought in the War of Independence upon the side of Bruce. The influence of the elder branch, at the time of which we write, was strongest in Northumberland and Cumberland, and of this line Sir Philip Somervyle was the tenth and last male representative. In October 1340 he gave, with the approval and advice of Richard Bury, the advowson of Mickle Benton in Northumberland, and two plough-lands within the same parish, to the Principals and Scholars of Balliol. As the purposes of the gift and the conditions attached to it were somewhat complicated, he persuaded the Principal and Scholars to let him draft a new code of Statutes. The original of these Statutes has long since disappeared from the archives, but we fortunately possess a copy, made only four years later, when Edward Balliol, as the representative of the original founders, gave his sanction to the changes which Somervyle had introduced. These were very considerable; it is hard to understand the worthy knight's protestation that his intent is not to destroy the ancient laws, but rather to confirm them. The only possible explanation is that the majority of his reforms had reference to the new arrangements already inaugurated by Felton, and would not affect the sixteen scholars of the old foundation.

It appears then that the Principal and Scholars had so far anticipated the resources of Abboldesley as to pension a small number of graduates, all former Scholars of the House, and all students of Divinity. Sir Philip enacted that they should be six in number, elected by the House. In making an election the Scholars were to choose men who were "upright, pure, peaceful, humble, having ability for the pursuit of learning and a desire to make progress." These were to be provided for out of the existing endowment. The bounty of Sir Philip Somervyle was to be employed partly in raising the allowances to twelvepence a week, as Felton had intended, and partly in endowing new places. There was to be a second chaplain, nominated by the Somervyle family, or in their default by the College. Six new Scholarships were to be created for students in arts, who were put on the same footing as the sixteen of the old foundation, except that the right of electing them was vested in the College, and that natives of Mickle Benton were to have the preference over those from other parts of the country.

The admission of these new inmates made necessary some important reforms in the constitution of the College. Sir Philip did not venture to destroy the old offices of the Principal and Procurators. But he reduced the former to insignificance by providing for the election of a graduate Master whom all members of the College were to obey, and he named, as colleagues of the Procurators, the Chancellor of the University, the Warden of Durham College and the Bishop of Durham.

The exact distribution of powers among these several authorities cannot be accurately determined from his Statutes; in fact, the Statutes were regarded as unintelligible and impracticable within a very few years from their promulgation. The Visitors quarrelled among themselves and with the College. The Principal and the Scholars of the old foundation might fairly claim that they were under no sort of obligation to obey the new Master, as Somervyle had commanded. Somervyle had provided that, if anything in his Statutes was contrary to the Statutes of Dervorguilla, then the older rule should prevail. If this principle had been consistently applied there would then have been under the same roof two distinct communities, governed by different authorities, enjoying totally separate endowments. Fortunately things never came to this pass. Again there was a compromise, made this time through the mediation of a Papal legate. In 1364 the College addressed a petition to Urban V. at Avignon, in which they represented that

"these enactments, though they are reasonable and useful to the College, and made as it is believed with a pious intention, are yet very contrary to the earlier Statutes, which in many ways troubles and disquiets the consciences of the Scholars, causes dissensions, and acts as an incentive to quarrels."

At the Pope's command, Simon Sudbury, Bishop of London, undertook to "modify, correct, withdraw or change" those of the Statutes which appeared to be contrary to the intentions of the original founders. Although of the revision thus made there is no copy in the archives, it is tolerably certain that Sudbury put an end to dissensions by abolishing, on the one hand the Visitatorial Board of Somervyle, and on the other the too democratic office of Principal. The Procurators regained most of their old powers, except that they ceased to interfere directly in the management of the property, and that an appeal lay henceforth from their decisions to the Bishop of London. The authority of the Master over the inmates and the belongings of the House remained substantially as it had been fixed by Somervyle. All elections were made by the general assembly of the College, except where one of Dervorguilla's sixteen scholarships were vacant. Here the Visitors retained their ancient right. For his administration of the College property the Master was accountable in the first instance to the same assembly. For all offences against discipline the court of first instance was composed of the Master and the two Senior Fellows. Thus the right of self-government was in a great measure conceded. This was the first grand result of the Somervyle Statutes. The second was the establishment of a graduate element in the College. The constitution was and remained for some time a democracy. The special advantages enjoyed by the graduates were few. If in a contested election to the Mastership the votes were equally divided, then the voice of the *sanior pars* was to prevail. If an offender had to be tried before the Master, then his assessors were taken from among the graduates. Of Commoners there is no trace at this period. They were probably introduced for the first time in the fifteenth century. As a matter of course, they had no voice in College meetings. But between the undergraduate Scholars of either foundation and the graduate Theologians little or no distinction was drawn.

There are few lighter touches to be found in the Somervyle Statutes. The most interesting sections are those which relate to the choice and the duties of a Master. The forms prescribed for the election have in part survived to our own day. The votes were received and written down by the Principal and two Scrutators, who sat apart in the Chapel, while the voters waited outside and entered one by one in order that secrecy might be preserved. The newly elected Master took an oath before the Senior Fellow that he would observe all the Statutes and Ordinances. He was then sent to call upon the lord for the time being of the manor of Wichnor; the lord was bound to confirm the election without further demur. After this two or three of the senior Fellows took the Master and introduced him to the Visitors.

In virtue of his station the Master had the privilege of a private room, and one servitor was always assigned to him. The latter practice remained in use until servitors were abolished in the College. It is not uncommon to find in the Admission Books a note that so and so is admitted "ad famulitium magistri." As it would be often necessary to entertain strangers coming on business, the Master might have "a table in no way luxurious, at the common expense," prepared for their delectation in the privacy of his own apartment. His duties are no less minutely described. Once a year he ought in person or by deputy to make a progress over the College estates and to prepare for the audit meeting an exact account of their condition. He received the rents, defrayed all current expenses, and handed over the surplus to the Treasurer by whom the chest was kept. Apart from the guardianship of the chest, the only financial duty which he deputed to a delegate was that of paying the allowances due to those upon the Somervyle foundation. The Somervyle Scholars were paid by "their Masters." We have here the first allusion to anything in the shape of a tutorial system. Apparently each of the six additional Scholars for whom Somervyle had provided was assigned as a pupil to one of the six theologians. There may have been already a similar arrangement for those upon the old foundation, but, so far as we know, Bishop Fox was the first to enact that every Scholar must have a tutor, and the Commoners were left to select tutors for themselves until 1587, or even later.

The Master could be deposed if his accounts were held to be unsatisfactory when inspected at the audit-meeting; or if he were "useless or negligent in fulfilling his office or luxurious or notoriously vicious." When the College wished to be rid of him, the Principal, or, after the abolition of that office, the Senior Fellow, would convene an indignation meeting. If the meeting declared in favour of strong measures the convener then delivered a solemn warning to the delinquent Head. If the warning had no effect it should be repeated a second and a third time. After the third warning the Master might, if still incorrigible, be denounced to the Visitors, who were then bound to remove him from his office without delay. Happily we know of no occasion on which the *ultima ratio* was found necessary.

The inferior members of the House were liable to punishment in different degrees. The Master and his assessors could inflict corporal punishment or an imposition; at a much later period "a sound swingeing" is mentioned as a natural if regrettable incident in the career of a Scholar. Contumacious offenders might be discommonsed for a fortnight, and when this punishment had been thrice inflicted without result, expulsion was permissible. Every Scholar took an oath on entering the House that he would never dispute a sentence of expulsion in a court of law; and it was the soundest policy to respect the oath, for the sentence of expulsion might be, and usually was, reversed if signs of contrition were remarked. The possible offences which Somervyle enumerates are a curious index to the moral standards of mediæval Oxford. Among those of a venial kind he notices the practice of shirking lectures and disputations, wandering in the city or outside it at unlawful times, misbehaviour at table, rudeness to a senior. But perjury, sacrilege, murder, adultery, theft and robbery, a quarrelsome disposition, assault and battery committed on the person of a Master or Scholar, and the fomenting of discord are bracketed together as deserving instant and condign punishment by way of perpetual exclusion.

That the society would be a poor one is the expectation and also the wish of the lawgiver. Should the revenues be increased at any future time the surplus is to be expended not on increasing the value of existing scholarships, but on founding others. The possession of an income of five pounds' clear annual value disqualified for a Fellowship; for the Master the maximum allowed was forty pounds. To exclude the merely avaricious it was directed that every Fellow[*] should take an oath on his admission that he would not attempt to procure his own election at another College where the stipend was higher.

Such then was the state of the College in Wyclif's time. His connection with Balliol has been already mentioned, and slight as it was some account must be given of the facts, and the conjectures which have been grounded upon them.

(1) Wyclif the Reformer held, at one time in his life, the benefice of Fillingham. This was in the gift of Balliol. It was one of three which Thomas Cave of Welwyk bequeathed in the year 1343, "that the number of Scholars might be increased." They served this purpose by offering to the Master and the Scholars one of those "competent ecclesiastical preferments" which entailed the vacation of a place. They could hardly be bestowed upon an outsider, even if the College were inclined to be so disinterested. (2) In the Balliol archives are certain documents of the years 1360 and

---

[*] The Statutes use the terms *Socius* and *Scholaris* interchangeably, and we have followed them in their inconsistency. The term *Socius* is not confined to graduates till Foxe's Statutes came into force.

1361, in which John de Wyclyff, Wyckclyffe, Wyclyffe, or Wyclyfe, appears as the Master, and transacts business on behalf of the College. This Master had been elected since 1356, in which year the office was held by Robert Derby*; he has disappeared from the scene by 1366, when John Hugate is named as Master. The presumption is that the Reformer is the person named in 1360 and 1361, and that he subsequently accepted the living of Fillingham. (3) The chain of evidence is strengthened when we remark that the living of Wyclif-upon-Tees, which was in the gift of the Reformer's family, was held by three members of Balliol in succession between the years 1363 and 1369. (4) It is tolerably certain that if the Reformer was Master of Balliol, as we have seen reason to believe, then he must at some time in his career have been a Scholar of the House. This condition of eligibility, though not expressly stated in the Somervyle Statutes, is certainly implied. The electors are charged to take that man " whom they *know* to have most knowledge and ability, and *most zeal for advancing the interests of the House.*" Until the year 1433 it was held that this clause, while not necessarily limiting the choice to present members of the House, did disqualify one who had never belonged to it. It does not follow that Wyclif the Reformer matriculated from Balliol ; he may have been for a time in some other College, though there is no evidence to prove the fact. Neither does it follow that Wyclif was resident within the House as a Graduate Theologian at

---

* Lechler says William Kyngston. This is an obvious error. Kyngston was Rector of Abboldesley, and Wyclif is called his successor when he takes over the rectory.

the time of his election to the Mastership; all we can say is that he might naturally be looked for in a House specially intended for the adversaries of the regular clergy. Could we prove the fact we should have established a still closer connection than is already known to have existed between the Reformer and Richard of Armagh, whose hand is so plainly to be traced in the Somervyle Statutes. But Wyclif may, so far as the Balliol evidence goes, have migrated on graduation to Merton or elsewhere, and have returned, after an interval of some years, to take up the mastership.

How many John Wyclifs there may have been we do not undertake to say with certainty, though we incline to the simplest hypothesis. A John Wyclif was steward of the week at Merton in 1356, which implies that he was a Fellow of some little standing. In July 1361 a John Wyclif was collated to the living of Mayfield by Simon Islip (himself a Merton man). In April 1365 Islip, being then ill at Mayfield, appointed "John Wyclyve" Warden of Canterbury Hall. Presumably the same Wyclif is meant in all three transactions. There is nothing to prevent us from identifying him with the Reformer and the Master of Balliol. The Reformer is last mentioned as Master of Balliol in April 1361. He may have come to Balliol from Merton, and may have gone from Merton to Mayfield. He could hold Mayfield and Fillingham together.

Simon of Islip was likely to be interested in a College which aimed at becoming a home of secular theologians. As a matter of fact, he was interested in Felton's donation to Balliol, for he appears as a witness to one of the deeds* concerning it. Moreover Canterbury Hall was to be a College of the same kind as Balliol. It was natural, therefore, that Islip should invite a Master of Balliol to undertake the reorganisation of Canterbury Hall. That the Reformer was Warden of Canterbury Hall is stated in set terms by his enemy, Wodeford. Wodeford advanced the statement with the definite purpose of blackening Wyclif's motives for preaching reform. But Wodeford was not a wholly unscrupulous controversialist, and Wyclif speaks of him with distinct respect. He was also an Oxford man who had come into personal contact with Wyclif, and was therefore in a position to know the facts about Canterbury Hall. On the whole, it is difficult not to accept his statement; Lechler has already done so. Those who aim at establishing the existence of two or three Wyclifs appear to be moved, either by a fear of admitting something to the discredit of the great Reformer, or by a mistaken impression as to the tenor of the Balliol Statutes.

We may add, by way of postscript, that the portrait of Wyclif in Balliol Hall, though often copied, is not an original nor, probably, a faithful likeness. The portrait now generally accepted as the most authentic is in the possession of King's College, Cambridge, and shows a stronger, sterner face.

* *Archives*, A 19. Deed of grant of Abbotsley to Balliol College. Dated from Newcastle-on-Tyne (1340). The name is spelt "Symon de Isleppe."

CHAPTER III

THE RENAISSANCE AND THE OLD LIBRARY

Masters: William Lambert, 1406; Thomas Chace, 1412; Robert Burley, 1428; Richard Stapylton, 1429; William Brandon, 1429; Robert Thwaytes, 1450; William Lambton, 1461; John Segden, 1472; Robert Abdy, 1477; William Bell, 1496.

A CLOUD of obscurity hangs over the history of Oxford in the fifteenth century. The annalists have little to tell us of this period, and that little is not interesting. The perennial feuds of regulars and seculars, Northerners and Southerners, artists and jurists ran their wonted course, and occasionally we find reason to suspect that older differences were aggravated by the jealousies of Lancastrian and Yorkist. The battles, however, were fought in the streets and not in the schools; they were excited less by conflicting ideas than by conflicting interests. In this age the Universities of Europe played a great *rôle* and accepted a great responsibility. Moved by vague premonitions of an approaching cataclysm, their leaders raised the cry for Catholic reform, and in two general Councils at Constance and at Bâle, waged battle over this question with the unsympathetic Curia. If they failed in their main enterprise, they were at least successful in vindicating the claims of the national

Churches to partial independence of Rome. But in their rebuffs and in their triumphs Oxford had very little part. The brunt of the struggle was born by the University of Paris. The reviving national spirit of the French had its effect even in the world of thought, and the failure of our arms in France appeared to paralyse the energies of our students at home.

There were other and deeper causes for the insignificance of Oxford at this period. The liberality of such benefactors as Archbishop Chicheley and Humphrey, Duke of Gloucester, could not compensate for the fall in value of agricultural estates. The University offered few substantial rewards to the ambitious student, and at the most he would use her distinctions as a stepping-stone to higher preferment. Even from this point of view a connection with Oxford seemed a dubious advantage. In 1438 the Masters of Arts addressed a querulous petition to Chicheley, the gist of which is that Oxford men are regarded with suspicion by those in whom Church patronage is vested. Under the Lancastrian kings England was governed by an aristocracy who, amid all their variances, remained unanimous in abhorrence of novel speculations, and particularly of those associated with the name of Wyclif. Oxford, the nursery of the Lollard movement, still counted among her sons an obscure but obstinate minority who pored over the pages of the *Wicket*, and criticised in a hostile spirit the fundamental doctrines of the mediæval Church. The authorities were unflagging in their attempts to uproot the handful of tares, but the reproach remained, and a generation must elapse before the University could regain her reputation for orthodoxy.

Accordingly, those of her sons who rose to great positions at this time were precisely those who for one reason or another had formed but a temporary connection with their Alma Mater. Most of them, indeed, were the scions of great families who treated Oxford as the half-way house to an Italian University, living for a year or two within her walls under the nominal supervision of a College tutor, but otherwise enjoying a complete immunity from the rules to which their social inferiors were subjected. The collegiate system had even less influence upon them than upon the Gentlemen-Commoners of later times, for these latter did at least live under the roof of a College and associate with the Fellows at high-table and in common-room. In the fifteenth century the University spared no pains to win the gratitude of her more influential pupils. She had no scruple whatever in conferring the highest honours in her gift upon youths not yet out of their teens, if anything might be hoped from their generosity. The ties thus created were slight in their character; the pupils so highly favoured passed out into the great world and soon forgot their Oxford life. The students of humbler birth, who had been really formed and educated in Oxford, seldom deserved or found an opportunity of carrying into public life the lessons which they had learned from her.

Still it is not the sole business of a University to produce public men. For this or any other career men cannot be successfully trained except in an atmosphere of intellectual pursuits. That atmosphere Oxford had lost in the reaction which followed upon the turmoil of the fourteenth century. It was necessary to open new fields of study, to create new standards of taste, and to start new trains of thought. Either from within or from without there must come the impulse towards a revolution of the English mind and a destruction of the chains with which it had been shackled by the schoolmen. Slowly, languidly, by imperceptible degrees, the need of change came to be felt in Oxford, and some idea was formed of the lines upon which change ought to proceed. The fifteenth century was here a period of preparation for the Renaissance in England. Among those who led the way in the new movement, the more prominent were Balliol men, and the story of the College at this time throws a gleam of light upon one of the least understood and the most interesting passages in our national history.

As a Northern College Balliol had special claims upon the favour of the Yorkist faction. Durham College being a monastic foundation, designed to promote the scientific study of theology, was less fitted to be the training-school of fashionable youth; Queen's, the other possible competitor, was deeply tainted with the Lollard heresy. If the sons of Yorkist nobles came at all to Oxford they entered their names upon the Balliol books. This did not mean that they resided. The noble undergraduate ordinarily hired a hostel for himself and his train. He took to himself a tutor from among the Fellows of his College, but the contract was a private one, and the tutor had only that amount of authority which the pupil and his parents were prepared to allow. Commoners of this class could if they pleased make their appearance at the disputations in their College Hall, but there was no compulsion and no inducement to make them pursue the hackneyed course. Still membership of a College was advantageous to them and to the society which they joined. They obtained a footing in a cultivated circle, and the College was the richer by the fees which they paid for the privilege. The latter fact was immediately comprehended by the Balliol authorities. They encouraged the inrush of Commoners to such good purpose that they were enabled to rebuild the whole of the quadrangle; when the treasure chest was empty they appealed, not in vain, to the Grays and the Nevilles and the Tiptofts to whom they had extended hospitality. The work which was begun with the fees was completed with the benefactions of the Commoners.

Time has left us few of these improvements. They have in their turn been improved out of existence; they can only be described from books and engravings. The builders began at the east side of the quadrangle. Then the Old Hall was erected; then the lower or western half of the Old Library; then the Master's House; and then the eastern part of the Old Library. Finally, at the end of the century, the block of buildings which faced Broad Street was entirely re-cast. A gateway, with a beautifully vaulted roof and a low tower above it, was inserted in the centre of the block. To complete the College, as we see it in Loggan's print, only a new Chapel was needed, and this was raised on the eve of the Reformation.

The front of the College has been entirely rebuilt, although the plan of the original gateway is in a manner preserved; of the Master's House only the shell has been spared. The interior of the Old Hall is transformed by the insertion of bookshelves, desks and tables in every available corner, by the destruction of the vaulted roof, and by the removal of the fireplace from the centre to the west side. The chambers underneath the Library have been made into common-rooms for the Fellows. The Library itself was retouched, though to a less degree, early in this century. Fortunately the architect, with something more than his usual amount of discretion, preserved the salient features of the building with which he had to deal, and after all changes it still remains a worthy memorial of the age which planned and carried out the design of the Divinity Schools. The ceiling is now defaced with whitewash and stucco. The richly blazoned windows, which Anthony Wood saw and described, survive only in fragments. St. Catharine with her wheel, the Fellows with their tonsures and "formalities" kneeling in adoration before her, the coats of arms, the jingling Latin mottoes which adorned every pane are gone. The space formerly occupied by the east window is concealed by bookshelves. St. Catharine is there, indeed, but only as a wooden effigy of the age of Laud. All these losses must be admitted. But in spite of them the room retains enough of its pristine beauty to show how completely the architects appreciated the ideals of the humanists by whom they were commissioned, the scholars who held with Plato that learning should be always shrined in beauty. The Old Library and the books which it contains must be our starting-point in dealing with this era.

Of the men who built the Library and the rest of the old College there is not much to be said. The Masters

From a Photograph by the] *[Oxford Camera Club*
THE OLD LIBRARY

of this period do not figure in the annals of their day, either as great scholars or as active politicians. Outside the University there was no opening for them. In their own narrow sphere they were the leaders of a movement which they comprehended at the best very dimly. Even as teachers they do not seem to have displayed more than ordinary abilities, and a moderate degree of ecclesiastical preferment kept them contented in the paddock of orthodoxy. It is enough then to say that the Master who began the restoration was Thomas Chace; * that after a long interval Thwaytes took up the work at the point where Chace had left it; and that the crowning efforts were made by Robert Abdy and by William Bell, whose good fortune it was to find among their former pupils a little band of wealthy and eager assistants. The best remembered names are those of Abdy and his friend Bishop Gray of Ely.

"Hos Deus adjecit, Deus his det gaudia cœli;
Hoc Abdy perfecit opus Gray praesul et Ely."

So ran the motto on the Library windows, which every reader of Wood will remember.

The books of which we have to speak are manuscripts, and the more interesting of them came from Italy in the middle of this era. Since the time of Felton, gifts of books had been not uncommon; there is a considerable list of volumes which are attributed in the Library catalogues to donors of the fourteenth century. But

---

* Chace was largely assisted by Richard Clifford, Bishop of London († 1421). The College said so many hard things of the Visitors at this time that it is a pleasure to find her under an obligation to one of them. Chace built the west or lower half of the Old Library.

this older nucleus of the Library belonged to a range of studies which were fast becoming obsolete. The Library was built less for their sake than for the books which the humanists were bringing into fashion. While the thunders of religious controversy were still rolling at Constance and at Bâle, Italy had put away theology from her affections. The example and precept of Petrarch fired the University of Padua with a new zeal for the study of the Latin classics. Encouraged first by the princely house of Carrara, and afterwards by the Venetian conquerors of that house, the professors of Padua proposed to their pupils as the final end and aim of education an ideal than which nothing could be more foreign to the mediæval spirit—"*Humanitas*, the pursuits and the activities proper to mankind," the complete development of the characteristic human faculties. The new spirit rapidly radiated from Padua through all the chief Italian cities. In 1397 there appeared in Florence the Byzantine professor, Chrysoloras; and from this "old man eloquent" the Italians suddenly learned that in the literature of classical Greece the most mature expression of the new ideal was to be found. In the company of Chrysoloras Italian scholars voyaged to Constantinople, ransacked the libraries on the shores of the Bosphorus, and learned to know Greek as a living language. Those who remained at home caught the inspiration from the travellers. In every princely court and merchant republic the humanists found lavish patrons and attentive audiences. The demand for classical education called into being a race of great teachers among whom some, such as Guarino da Verona, were fired by a purely intellectual fervour and aimed at creating a race of exact scholars, while others holding to the more liberal precepts of Vittorino da Feltre aspired to form in their pupils the character of the perfect citizen, and to develop the moral and æsthetic in equal measure with the reasoning faculties.

By the year 1430 the movement had become of more than Italian importance. The humanists, with a regal contempt for national prejudice and pecuniary emolument, scattered their stores of learning broadcast among hearers of all countries and all social ranks. A new theory of education was moulded in their lecture-rooms and reduced to a system in widely circulated treatises. Tradition makes the Italian Renaissance begin with the conquest of Constantinople by the Turk in 1453; but long before that time the new learning had made a triumphal entry into Western Europe. England, longer than other countries, remained unaffected by the change. Returning for a moment from Italy to Balliol, we find recorded in the Library Catalogue certain donations by Robert Stapylton, who was Master for a short while in 1429. The Library was now half completed, and becoming aware that erudition was in vogue, the old gentleman bestowed the most precious contents of his bookshelves on the College "in perpetuum exemplum ut magistri et socii conformiter faciant et multo melius si poterint." The present, intended for an example to posterity, consisted of two volumes. The first was a commentary on the *Libri Sententiarum*, the *vade mecum* of the old-fashioned theologian. The other was a commonplace book containing anecdotes—the gleanings of much discursive reading and many convivial nights;

also a list of "various remedies for various diseases." It is a thousand pities that no Erasmus was then alive to give us his impressions of this worthy Master. Robert Thwaytes, the next benefactor on the list, was hardly more modern in his tastes. To him the Library was indebted for a copy of the *Perils of the Latter Times*, by William of St. Amour, which had made some stir two hundred years before, but had now fallen to the rank of a harmless literary curiosity; also for a sermon against the Friars Minor by a monk of Durham College. But there is a third and more striking example of persistent conservatism. The Library contains an odd volume of *Duns Scotus*, presented by Mr. Alexander Bell, a contemporary of Thwaytes. On the fly-leaf Bell has written down a list of the books in his possession, with notes of the prices which he gave for some of them. The list does credit to his zeal for learning; between thirty and forty works of a solid character are mentioned, and they all appear to have been expensive. But without exception they are old-fashioned; even the scientific and mathematical books which he names might have belonged to a disciple of Roger Bacon.

Thwaytes and Bell were sadly in the rear of the age. In Balliol all the younger men were humanists by the year 1450; some of them were making their literary pilgrimage to Italy, and gathering together books which would give the College Library an altogether new aspect. Of these pilgrims Gray, afterwards Bishop of Ely, has the largest claim upon our gratitude. Attracted, like the majority, by the scholarship of Guarino much more than by the moral discipline of Vittorino, he visited Ferrara, where the Veronese was now permanently established as the tutor of the Este family. Guarino's teaching had at least the result of inducing Gray to collect one of the finest libraries which had been seen north of the Alps. This work he carried to its completion during the five years (1449–1454) which he spent at Rome as Proctor to Henry VI. No book came amiss to him, for he had been trained by a master wholly free from the narrow purism of the later humanists. Guarino valued patristic literature for the side-lights which it threw upon the social life of the ancient world; he also encouraged the study of universal history, on the ground that nothing so enlarges the mind as familiarity with the manners and institutions of many epochs and many nations. Accordingly in Gray's collection Augustine elbowed Cicero, Higden and Capgrave[*] found an honourable place beside Plutarch and the historians of the later Roman Empire. In all there were more than two hundred volumes of every date from the twelfth century to the fifteenth. The most beautiful were those transcribed expressly for the collector; in many cases these were illuminated for him by "that exquisite painter, Antonius Marius" of Florence. Among the authors represented were Lysias, Plato, Aristotle, Vergil, Seneca, Quintilian, Petrarch, Poggio Bracciolini, and Grey's own master, Guarino.

This collection passed at the death of Gray (1478) to the Balliol Library, for, owing to his friendship with

---

[*] The College possesses the autograph copy of Capgrave's chronicle; also his *Commentary on the Acts of the Apostles*, dedicated to Bishop Gray; also his treatise on the Creed with autograph corrections.

Robert Abdy, the Bishop never ceased to entertain close relations with his old College, and he had a special interest in the Library, to the building of which he had contributed considerable sums of money. His books are still the chief treasures of the Library. According to the excellent catalogue of Mr. Coxe there remain about one hundred and fifty volumes which are known to have been included in his gift. A number were destroyed by the Edwardian Reformers, and of the rest many have been barbarously defaced by the excision of the illuminated initial letters. These vandalisms are noted by Anthony Wood, but he is unable to tell us by whom they were perpetrated. Perhaps we shall not be far wrong in attributing them to the later sixteenth century. It was even then the rule that no one should enter the Library except in the company of a Fellow, and therefore, even if we hold the Masters and Fellows personally innocent, we cannot but tax them with the grossest negligence. Since the Restoration all the manuscripts have been guarded with the most scrupulous care, and there is no reason for thinking that anything of importance has been lost or stolen in the last two hundred years. The following volumes at least may be recommended to visitors as worthy of inspection:*

No. VI. St. Augustine. *Homilies* on the Fourth Gospel (sacc. xii.).

No. XVII. *Commentary on Jeremiah*, by Hugh of St. Caro, with the armorial bearings of Bishop Gray on the first page (sacc. xv.).

* The numbers given are those of Coxe's catalogue.

No. LXIV. *Commentary on the Sentences*, by Peter of Candia (sacc. xiv.).

No. CXXV. A volume of the later Latin Historians (sacc. xv.).

No. CXLIV. St. Chrysostom. Miscellaneous writings (1447).

No. CCXXXII. Aristotle. Miscellaneous writings (sacc. xiv.).

There is abundance of evidence to prove that the studies pursued by Gray were not peculiar to himself. Though Gray was the most considerable of Balliol humanists, there are others who live in the pages of history. Tiptoft, "the Butcher of England," had studied at the feet of Guarino, and acquired the reputation of a literary amateur, long before he became infamous for his share in the atrocious feuds of the Roses. If the first to introduce martial law in England, he was also the munificent patron of the printer Caxton. Lord Berners, the translator of Froissart, and, at the very end of the century, Cuthbert Tunstal, were for at least a short time members of the College. The deficiency of records belonging to this time must make us chary of mentioning individual names. But in the time of Wood there was a generally received tradition that Balliol had been during the Renaissance the nursery of the noble youth of England; and the author of the *Athenae* did not hesitate to bestow upon Balliol any Oxford men of eminence, such as Duke Humphrey and Sir Thomas More, to whom no other College could establish an authentic claim. His conjectures have little value. But there are two humanists more certainly connected with the College whom we cannot refrain from noticing, rather because their careers indicate a revolution in the spirit of the resident Fellows, than because their attainments were in themselves remarkable. John Free, elected a Fellow about the middle of the century, was a poor man of obscure family. But he scraped together the funds to transport himself to Italy and settled down at Padua to pursue the studies of medicine and natural science. There is still to be seen in the Balliol Library a Natural History of his composition, entitled *Cosmographia Mundi cum naturis arborum, plantarum, specierum diversarum*. Less brilliant than some of his contemporaries, he had the advantage of them in a reputation for stainless orthodoxy. This, together with a well-timed dedication, commended him to the notice of the austere Paul II., through whose favour he obtained the benefice of St. Michael in the Mount, Bristol. Immediately afterwards he was designated to the vacant See of Bath and Bristol, but died within a month *non sine veneni suspicione* (1465), leaving behind him a name for solid learning, and twenty volumes of original writings which the world has conspired to forget. Free's friend and correspondent, John Gunthorpe, had a longer and more prosperous career. He was one of those fortunate individuals who rose at this time from comparative obscurity to a position of honour and affluence through no other merit than that of possessing a Ciceronian style. He went to Italy about the same time as Free, and became the favourite pupil of Guarino. On his return to England Edward IV. made him a royal chaplain and employed him as an orator on several state-occasions, notably at the wedding of his sister Margaret, when Gunthorpe was selected to pronounce a panegyric on the bridegroom, Charles of Burgundy. For these and similar services he was rewarded with the Deanery of Wells, and in 1483 promoted to be keeper of the Privy Seal. Henry VII. afterwards forgave his services to the Yorkist cause and employed him as an envoy at the courts of Spain and Burgundy. Thus, remarks Leland with unconscious humour, did his literary attainments make him *tantum non immortalem*.

Among those benefactors who are less intimately connected with the literary movement, George Neville, the brother of the King-maker, is the most conspicuous. He graduated from Balliol in the year 1452. The event is dear to antiquarians, from Anthony Wood downwards, on account of the entertainment with which it was celebrated. Like the "swarry" of the Bath footmen, immortalised by the presence of Mr. Samuel Weller, this entertainment took a most substantial form. A supper was the invariable epilogue to any kind of examination; the practice led to such outrageous extravagance that the University was compelled to interfere, and Bishop Fox, in his Statutes for Balliol, forbids a B.A. to spend more than ten or an M.A. more than twenty shillings on such occasions. But George Neville was too great a man to be bound by sumptuary laws; the like of his feast had never been seen in Oxford. The tables were laid on two successive days; on the first there were six hundred covers, on the second three hundred, " for the entertainment only of Scholars and certain of the Proceeder's relations and acquaintances." This lavish hospitality did not go unrewarded. In the following year George Neville was elected

Chancellor of the University, though barely twenty years of age. The only excuse for this excessive servility on the part of Congregation is that the Pope himself followed the example. In 1456 George Neville received the See of Exeter with a dispensation to remain a layman for the space of four years. In 1464 he became Archbishop of York. His subsequent career by no means justified this rapid advancement, and, indeed, gives us a very low opinion of his character. He turned against his patron Edward IV., and took a prominent part in the temporary restoration of Henry VI. Then after Barnet Field he endeavoured to retrieve his fortunes by an abject submission to his brother's conqueror. Edward respected the sacred office of the captive so far as to grant him his life, but the former favourite of fortune languished for the remainder of his days in ignominious obscurity.

It is with more pleasure that we turn to John, Cardinal Morton, who had at least the redeeming virtue of honesty. Born about the year 1420, Morton came to Balliol, from the monastic school of Cerne Abbas in Dorsetshire, at a comparatively advanced age. Having little or no family influence he resigned himself to an academic career and became a distinguished member of the Law Faculty. In 1446 Thwaytes, the Master of Balliol, on being appointed to the office of Chancellor, nominated Morton as his Commissary, and other allusions in the archives of the University prove that Morton's administrative abilities received their first training in this narrow field. University business was not then conducted in the most pacific way, as the future Cardinal discovered to his cost. Questions of precedence arose between the Faculties of Arts and Law, and wounded honour on both sides resorted to the arguments of sticks and stones. It was impossible for the least bellicose to avoid these affrays; we are not surprised to find, in 1447, that William Vowell and Edmund Martyr were haled into the Court of the Commissary (or Vice-Chancellor) and ordered to pay 33s. 4d. to John Morton "for medicaments and the labours of his doctor, and for his hurts and injuries." Morton may well have rejoiced when a Dorsetshire patron presented him to a tranquil parish in his native county. But he carried away into retirement something of the party spirit of Oxford life. His services to the Lancastrians during the next few years were so pronounced that in 1461 they drew down upon his devoted head a sentence of attainder from a Yorkist Parliament. He escaped the block, and afterwards won the favour of Edward IV., who could not afford to slight the services of a distinguished lawyer. Thenceforth Morton's promotion was rapid, but he never lost touch with the University to which he owed his start in life. His academic friends on their side watched his career with pride. His disgrace under Richard III. elicited an eloquent protest from the Masters assembled in Convocation. "The bowels of our brother the University, like Rachael weeping over her children, were moved with pity at the distress of this her dearest son." At the close of his career, in 1494, Morton was elected Chancellor of the University, and repaid the honour by generous benefactions. He gave money towards the Divinity Schools, and assisted in the completion of the University Church. It is disappointing to find that he did nothing for his own College. Balliol owes far more to his friend and colleague, Fox, yet upon Fox she had no claims of gratitude.

Of the social life of the College during this period we have to form an idea chiefly from the notices of ancient customs in the later registers, and from the Statutes which the University framed for the Halls about the year 1489. We find that great attention was paid to questions of precedence. The Doctor took a higher rank than the Master of Arts; both were immeasurably superior to the Bachelor and the mere Undergraduate. Unless he were of noble birth, the latter was treated very much as a schoolboy; the pettiest details of his conduct were regulated by legislation. In the Halls Saturday night was fixed as the regular time for flogging those who had committed serious breaches of discipline, such as playing dice, quarrelling or brawling, bringing dogs and hawks within the gates, or behaving with insolence to the tutors. Fines were imposed for lesser offences, among which are specially mentioned those of rioting in Hall, spilling meat or drink on the tablecloth, throwing the rushes about the floor, cutting one's name upon the walls or tables. The most innocent amusements, such as tennis, chess, and fencing, are rigidly forbidden.

On the other hand, all ranks were so much thrown together in the course of daily life, that the College must have borne some resemblance to a large family. The Scholars voted at College meetings. The two principal meals of the day were regularly taken in Hall. The private rooms were mere dormitories, and even for the graduates there can have been little solitary study.

Every one who was inclined to work resorted to the Library; it was impossible to carry away the books because they were chained to their desks. There was no hard and fast distinction between the servants and their masters. The former were usually matriculated members of the University; they took an oath on admission to observe all the Statutes of the foundation and to divulge no secrets; if they neglected their duties they were reprimanded, not by any single official or in private, but publicly by the same College meeting which dealt with recalcitrant Scholars. In spite of all formalities there was a certain primitive simplicity in College life. "Oxford fare" was a recognised synonym for the plainest of plain living; according to Sir Thomas More it was only one step downwards from that to the diet of the vagrant who sang his "Salve Regina!" from door to door, and filled his wallet with the broken meats of charity. Herbs and vegetables were grown in the College gardens; there seems to have been a curious rule that a small allotment should go with every private chamber. It was either the duty or the privilege of the individual to grow his own cabbages. We should err in regarding the Balliol men of the time as pinched with poverty. There is no warrant for connecting them with the time-honoured stories of poaching in Shotover, of fights with irate foresters, of robberies committed on the king's highway. But a society which depended upon northern rents as the main source of its income cannot have been affluent in the fifteenth century.

Among the most disagreeable incidents of University life the plague undoubtedly claims the pre-eminence of this time. It visited Oxford repeatedly in the last ten or fifteen years of the century, and the mortality which it caused was usually serious. Those colleges which could afford to do so migrated, during a visitation of the plague, to some village in the immediate neighbourhood of Oxford. It is quite possible that George Neville's gift to Balliol of the farm of Moreton near Tame was made with a view to providing a retreat of this kind. Bishop Fox in the Statutes of 1509 gives formal permission for such migrations, only stipulating that the new lodgings shall be within twelve miles of Oxford, and that some one shall remain behind to serve the College Chapel.

The pugnacity of the undergraduate appears to have increased rather than diminished since the days of Wyclif, and as the scene of conflicts was now generally in the northern suburbs rather than in the High Street, Balliol men probably had no lack of martial experiences. Beaumont and St. Giles had acquired a most undesirable reputation as the home of the more turbulent sort of undergraduate. His depredations were extended even so far afield as Yarnton and Woodstock. He was perpetually at feud with the more civilised community within the city walls. The University legislated with great severity to repress the evil; in 1432 a singularly minute tariff of fines was published, providing for almost every conceivable form of assault, and resembling nothing so much as an Anglo-Saxon table of wergilds. But the Vice-Chancellor's Court appears to have been suffering, like all other organs of administration throughout the country, from an intermittent paralysis. Fatalities were of frequent occurrence, and the perpetrators seldom met with adequate punishments. It was a quite unusual occurrence if the Royal Justices appeared upon the scene to make an inquiry respecting some more than usually outrageous riot.

CHAPTER IV

BISHOP FOX'S STATUTES

Masters: William Bell, 1496; Richard Barningham, 1504.

In the last chapter we forbore to speak of constitutional changes because those which meet our notice in the fifteenth century are important chiefly as signs of the future, and as a prelude to the legislation of Bishop Fox. It will be remembered that the Somervyle Statutes were revised, about twenty years after they were first drawn up, by Simon Sudbury, acting under a commission from the Pope; and that the chief alteration then made had reference to the Visitatorial authority. Simon Sudbury destroyed the new Board which Somervyle had created, and took away from the See of Durham the right of acting as a supreme court of appeal in the affairs of the College. He not only restored the Procurators to their old position of importance, but he gave them in addition the new right of controlling the Somervyle Foundation no less than that of Dervorguilla. He reserved to himself and his successors in the See of London the power of amending and adding to the Statutes as should appear convenient. Accordingly we find that the legislation of the fifteenth century emanates from the Bishop of London acting at the suggestion and under the guidance of the Procurators. For example, in 1433, on the report of John Feckyngton and Richard Roderham, Procurators, that certain changes in the conditions attached to the Mastership were desirable, the Bishop of London decreed that for the future the Master may continue to hold his office *quam diu se bene gesserit*, even though he has come into possession of a private income of more than £40; also that the Fellows at future elections to the Mastership may lawfully choose an outsider if they care to do so. So also in 1477 Bishop Kemp gave the Master permission to absent himself in term time for any good and sufficient purpose such as lecturing, disputing, or presiding at disputations. His duties during his absence were to be discharged by a Vicegerent.

These are the only Decrees of the century before Fox. That they were liberally supplemented by new customs we know. An entry of a later date in the Register tells us of customs which arose in connection with the appointment of a Vicegerent. He ought to be appointed by the Master and in the presence of a College meeting assembled in the Chapel. Only one of the three Senior Fellows was eligible. After choosing between them the Master ought to give the keys and the Statutes to his nominee. If this formality had been omitted, then the government, pending the Master's return, devolved upon the Senior Fellow.

These changes were far from being commensurate with the wishes of the College. If the petitions which the Scholars sent to Rome were seriously meant, relations with the Visitors must have been more than strained. It is possible that ill-will towards the Friars had something to do with the friction; for one of the Procurators was always a Franciscan. It seems more likely that the conservatism of the Procurators, quite apart from their profession, was their real offence. The object of Simon Sudbury had been conservative, to restore the Statutes of Dervorguilla in their old strictness. If the Procurators continued to rule the House in this spirit after the Renaissance had fairly begun, then, indeed, collisions were only to be expected. They might, for example, throw serious obstacles in the way of those who desired to enlarge the scope of their studies; they might tie the juniors down to their Priscian, and compel the graduates to read nothing but Theology.

Our information as to the grievance which the College had against its Visitors would be more precise did we possess the text of the petitions which it addressed to the Holy See in 1503 and 1504. We can, however, learn something of their contents from the replies vouchsafed to them. The Visitors are charged with raking up obsolete Statutes, which there is no good reason for observing, and with expelling Scholars who have not complied with these Statutes. Then we are told that in nominating to vacancies on the old foundation the Visitors paid no regard to the wishes of the College, but nominated absolute strangers, who busied themselves in stirring up quarrels and dissensions. It was true that the Scholars could appeal from the Procurators to the Bishop of London; but in their petitions they did not spare the character of the episcopal court. There had been, they said, a certain

Bishop who made unpopular changes and "fanned the flames of discord, which scattered the Master and Fellows, threw everything out of order, wasted the substance of the College, and nearly brought it to ruin." It is hard to tell from hearing only one side whether the College had been rudely checked in an enlightened attempt at self-reform, or whether it had been properly punished for wilful neglect of the Founder's intentions. But since the request for a change of government was granted there may have been some reasonable foundation for it.

The request was granted originally by Alexander VI. in the year 1503. He gave a commission to the Bishops of Norwich and Winchester, empowering them to make any changes in the College Statutes which they might think proper. But his death, following immediately afterwards, seems to have been regarded as invalidating the commission, and Balliol was therefore spared the necessity of inscribing a Borgia on her list of benefactors. In 1504 Julius II. granted a new commission of precisely the same extent as the first, to the Bishops of Winchester and Carlisle. It is hardly necessary to add that the Bishop of Winchester whom two successive Pontiffs selected for this work was Fox, the future founder of Corpus Christi College. That justly celebrated institution, the most complete product of the Renaissance spirit which Oxford possesses, was as yet a mere idea in the mind of the founder; but he was already known, even outside England, as a patron of humanism who still contrived to keep the first place in his affections for the Church.

Three years elapsed before the desired changes could

be introduced. The two Papal delegates had been empowered to act either jointly or separately, and the Bishop of Carlisle appears to have left his colleague a free hand. Consequently, the new Statutes which were at length issued bear the name of Fox alone. That he did not approach his duties without assistance we know. The College at his desire appointed Syndics to confer with him, and Claymond, at that time President of Magdalen and afterwards the Head of Fox's own College, gave his advice. If we compare the Statutes made for Balliol with those of Corpus Christi, it is obvious that Fox did not feel entitled to remodel an ancient foundation entirely according to his own ideas. Rather he thought it his duty to ascertain the intentions of the founders and to make a constitution of the kind best suited to fulfil those intentions. The new code is stamped with Fox's individuality; there is a definite and coherent design running through it, which contrasts very favourably with the vagueness and confusion of the earlier Statutes; but it is far from representing the ideal of a Renaissance foundation.

The changes which commended themselves to Fox and his advisers were briefly these. The graduate members of the House were to be left at liberty to pursue their studies in Philosophy and Theology; for it seemed absurd that the rules which Dervorguilla had made for young boys should be held to bind grown men, whose presence in the House she had never contemplated. It was desirable to emancipate the College from the Procurators and to place it under a more sympathetic and large-minded authority. It was desirable also that the number of scholars on the foundation should be reduced, since the revenues were insufficient to support the twenty-eight for whom Somerville's Statutes provided. Finally, there was every reason why the democratic element in the constitution should be abolished. The undergraduate Scholars were mere boys; the rules of the University placed them in a position of subjection to the Theologians; it was a mere anomaly that they should have a vote at College meetings. The idea of a College had been radically changed since the thirteenth century. It was no longer that of a society of equals linked together by the zeal for learning, but rather that of a finishing school, in which the discipline should be severe and subordination absolute. The pupils could no longer be allowed to govern their masters.

The new Statutes were a highly successful attempt to make these reforms without disturbing, more than was unavoidable, the continuity of social life and custom. Wherever possible the old usage was retained; in one or two cases the very words of previous Statutes are repeated by the old code. Fox introduced no new factors into the composition of the College. He was content to readjust the relations of those which he found already in existence, to sweep away some old distinctions which had lost their meaning, to recognise others which had won their way into custom, and in some few cases to create new ones. His cautious conservatism is nowhere more apparent than when he is dealing with the question of studies. Here he must have been sorely tempted to override the traditions and tendencies of the College, and to mitigate the predominance of theology. But he refrained, thinking, no doubt, that the society would derive more benefit from those studies to which they were naturally inclined than from a more liberal course, which they would only approach with reluctance and under constraint. All that he did was to prescribe a diligent application to the subjects which Somerville and the Lady Dervorguilla had selected; and to direct that the graduate Fellows should, in addition to their private reading, deliver lectures and take part in disputations.

His constitutional reforms, startling as they appear, were carefully adapted to pre-existent circumstances. There were already nine or ten members of the House who claimed a certain precedence of the rest, either on account of superior standing in the University or because of their official position within the House. He decreed that for the future there should always be ten such persons, all of them Bachelors, Masters, or Doctors, who were to be distinguished from the other inmates of the House by the title of Fellows, and in whose hands the whole of the government was to be vested. To each of them some definite duty was assigned; and all alike were to have a share in the tuition of the juniors. These latter were henceforth to be called *Scholastici* in contradistinction to the *Socii*. Their number was reduced from twenty-two to ten. Each of these ten was to be nominated by some one Fellow who supervised his education and was made generally responsible for his good conduct.

The House being thus reduced to the form of an aristocracy, the Master lost some of his old prerogatives, and sank to the position of a constitutional monarch surrounded by parliamentary ministers. In other words, the larger half of the administration is transferred to officials who are elected periodically at College meetings. Of these officials the most important are the Senior and Junior Bursars. Almost the whole management of the estates is to be left in their hands, and the ordinary expenditure of the House is regulated by them. The Master exercises a general supervision over them, and still makes his accustomed progress round the estates. But their chief responsibility is to the Fellows' Meeting before which they lay their annual statement of accounts at Luke-tide. Similarly the discipline of the House is on all ordinary occasions to be upheld by the Deans, the Master only interfering when exceptional offences have to be visited with exceptional penalties. The Senior Dean has also the sole charge of the Library; it is his duty to see that no stranger enters it unaccompanied by the Master or a Fellow, that silence and order are preserved among the readers, that the books are properly treated and kept in their places. The Junior Dean is in like manner responsible for the vestments, the plate, and the other property of the Chapel. The Chapel services are performed, as before, by two Chaplains who are counted among the ten Fellows, and except in respect of their peculiar duties stand upon precisely the same footing of authority and privileges as their colleagues. Finally, there is the Senior Fellow who is the guardian of the traditions of the House, the spokesman of the Fellows in all their dealings with the Master, and the usual Vicegerent whenever the Master has occasion to absent himself. But as the governing body is so small the obligation of residence is carefully enforced. The Fellows are only permitted to take one vacation of eight weeks during the year. The Master must reside not less than forty days in each term.

The Society, thus governed, is elaborately compared by the Bishop to a human body, in which all the members have their offices, and the lower are controlled by the higher. The servants are the feet of the body, whose function it is to go whither they are bidden. The Scholars for some obscure reason are the legs. The two Chaplains correspond to the ribs " quae spiritualia includant membra." The Bursars are the arms, the Deans are the shoulders. The Master is the head, and the Senior Fellow is the neck by which body and head are united into one whole. The functions of the Master are quaintly expressed, in accordance with the metaphor, as "seeing clearly, hearing discreetly, tasting moderately, touching in a suitable and becoming manner." The remaining Fellows perform the useful but undignified office of the stomach.

The whole Society is subjected to rigorous laws of discipline. The Fellows are compelled to take Orders or to resign within a limited period after attaining to the Master's degree; the *Scholastici* are tonsured, and wear a clerical garb. Thus the College assumes the aspect of a seminary, and this is the ideal by which the conduct of the residents is regulated. The *Scholastici* have to wait upon the Fellows at table; and they must content themselves with the broken meats which are left over when the Fellows have finished. During meals the Scriptures are read aloud, and all conversation is in Latin, except when some unlearned person has to be addressed. The gates of the College are locked at eight in the winter and nine in the summer; the keys are carried to the Master's Lodgings, where they remain in his custody till the following morning. The costume, the demeanour, and the destination of those who leave the College in the daytime are severely scrutinised. Bows and arrows, when carried for purposes of recreation, are permissible; other weapons, only when one is making a journey away from Oxford. No one, junior or senior, may enter a tavern, ale-house, or other such place of entertainment, unless, indeed, he is invited by some distinguished stranger whose wishes must be treated as commands. So, too, all are enjoined to shun indulgence in unseemly pastimes, and the society of strolling players, gleemen, and jugglers. Expenditure on feasts and entertainments is strictly limited. The Doctor of Divinity may spend 40s. above his commons, other men smaller sums proportionate to their standing. If any one, in the superabundance of his hospitality, wishes to exceed these limits, he must obtain special leave from the Master and Fellows.

Obstinate offenders against these and similar rules are sent by their Dean before the Master, who holds a court of inquiry, with one Dean, one Bursar, and two of the senior Fellows for assessors. An Undergraduate, if found guilty by this court, may be expelled; but in the case of a Graduate, the sentence must be first confirmed by the Visitor.

As a matter of course, Fox is careful to define the qualifications for admission to the Society. It was necessary that he should be particularly explicit since he had given to the College the sole and exclusive right of nominating to vacancies. His dread of corrupt influence at elections is attested by the provision that any candidate for a Fellowship or other place who canvasses the electors, or procures letters of recommendation from great persons, shall, *ipso facto*, be disqualified. Other precautions are added to this. For the office of Master only those are eligible who have passed the age of thirty, who have entered into priest's orders, who are learned in theology. The candidate for a Fellowship must be a Bachelor of Arts, *de legitimo thoro natus*, of good character, and proficient in his studies. His need of assistance must be genuine; any cure of souls, and a private income of more than 40*s.* a year, are held to disqualify. Subject to these rules the Fellowships are thrown open to competition; the only advantage given to Scholars of the College is that, *caeteris paribus*, they are to be preferred to strangers. As *Scholastici* may be nominated any persons who are of good character, less than eighteen years of age, and well skilled in grammar and plain-song.

Owing to the reduction in the numbers of the foundation it was possible for Fox to raise the allowances to the extent which the rise of prices required. The ordinary commons of a Fellow are now fixed at 1*s.* 4*d.* a week, which on the occasion of a greater festival is raised to 1*s.* 8*d.* In addition they receive small annual stipends, varying in amount according to their degree; for a Master of Arts the sum fixed is 28*s.* 8*d.*; for a Bachelor 18*s.* 2*d.* The Master in consideration of his onerous duties is entitled to 40*s.*; he has also the option of taking any College living which falls vacant, to be held concurrently with the Mastership; but he may not hold more than one such living at a time.

The only point that remained to be settled was the choice of a Visitor. Fox was warned by the previous history of the College, and did his best to make complaints about the Visitors impossible for the future. He swept away the extraneous Masters, and ignored the Bishops of London and Lincoln. He gave to the Master and Fellows the unique privilege of choosing their own Visitor, and enacted furthermore that the Visitor, unless expressly invited, should not be entitled to appear in the College more than once a year. The theoretical objections to such an arrangement are obvious, and although in our own century the Master and Fellows have amply justified the confidence which Fox reposed in their good-feeling and discretion, this has not been invariably the case. Some of the appointments made in the eighteenth century might justly be criticised; political considerations were then allowed to outweigh all others, and unfortunately the Fellows then adhered to a party which was woefully deficient in men of administrative ability. But on the whole the privilege has had few evil consequences, and the Visitors chosen by the College have rarely been wanting in good-will and impartiality. Oddly enough, nearly two centuries elapsed before the Master and Fellows ventured to exercise their new freedom of choice. There were difficulties with the Bishop of Lincoln, who claimed and exercised all the rights of an Ordinary; and, after the Reformation began, it became impossible to claim a privilege which ultimately rested on Papal authority. From 1540 onwards the right of the See of Lincoln was admitted without a murmur; and it received royal confirmation when the See of Oxford was founded. It is hardly to be accounted an exception that the office was conferred on Laud (1637–1643) when at the height of his power. The authority of Lincoln was for the first time repudiated in 1691, when Dr. Busby of Westminster was elected in consideration of his munificent gifts to the College. Since that time freedom of choice has been the rule. In the eighteenth century it was usual to elect a Bishop, or some other ecclesiastical dignitary; but in more recent times the choice of the College has fallen upon laymen.*

The College was now in possession of that Code by which it continued to be governed until the first University Commission of the present reign. Few changes of importance were made before the year 1800, and these were for the most part necessitated by the grafting of new foundations upon the College, or by the unexpected influx of Commoners. The great period of innovation was that from 1800 to 1850, and so thoroughly was the work of reform then effected that the Commissioners found little work to do, beyond abrogating in a formal manner those rules which had been allowed to fall into desuetude. It would, in fact, be an idle exercise of ingenuity to trace in Fox's Statutes the secret of the present prosperity of Balliol. Fox intended the College to be a theological seminary, and was so far successful that for three hundred years the divine was the most characteristic product of Balliol, and those of her sons who achieved eminence in other walks of life were for the most part men whose association with her had been of the most temporary kind.

* We print in an Appendix (No. II.) a complete list of Visitors so far as their names can be gathered from the College archives.

The Bishop perhaps did the best with the materials upon which he had to work, but no one can regret the piecemeal destruction of his constitution. The most successful part of his Code was undoubtedly that which provided for the administration of the College and its estates. In this direction he showed statesmanlike ability and educed order out of chaos. Still we should err if we supposed that there was a complete breach with the past of the College. Many things were left to be regulated by unwritten custom, and those who know the Balliol of to-day will recognise in the usages of the nineteenth century many traces of the fifteenth and the fourteenth. Previous historians of the College, and particularly Mr. Poole, in his interesting chapter contributed to Mr. Clarke's volume, have somewhat neglected to accentuate the continuity of its traditions. But in a small and conservative society changes are effected very slowly, and most often the legislator is only successful where he brings to the light of day new developments which have for a long time past been maturing in the unchronicled practice of every day.

CHAPTER V

THE OLD CHAPEL AND THE REFORMATION

Masters: Richard Stubbs, 1518; William Whyte, 1525; George Cootes, 1539; William Wryght, 1545; James Brookes, 1547; William Wryght, 1555; Francis Babington, 1559; Antony Garnett, 1560.

For some years after the framing of the Statutes a deep tranquillity overshadowed the College. If there were malcontents who deplored the recent changes we hear nothing of them. The only legislation which the Register records is a decree of the Master and Fellows, to clear up two doubtful points which Fox had left undecided. One was the amount of stipend to which a Fellow was entitled if he resigned at some other time than the end of the year; the second, what was to become of a Scholar when the Fellow by whom he was nominated resigned. On the latter head the decision was that

" it shall be lawful for any one of the Fellows to take him, without any readmission, as his Scholar for the time determined by the Statutes. . . . And if none of the Fellows shall see fit to place him among his company of Scholars, so that he be left destitute and wander like a fugitive over the earth, we permit him to provide for

OLD CHAPEL AND REFORMATION

himself assistance from all the goods and revenues of our Scholars for the space of not more than two months."

From 1521 to 1529 the one subject of attention was the new Chapel, with which it was now considered advisable to replace the oratory built in the reign of Edward III. The work was begun by Richard Stubbs, elected Master in 1518, and even after his retirement he continued, as Visitor of the College, to take a lively interest in his scheme. The site selected was due east of the Library, and in a line with it, so that the east wall of the Library with its great Catharine window served for a west end to the Chapel. The name of the architect is unknown to fame, but whoever he was, he succeeded in producing a design which harmonised completely with the general scheme of the front quadrangle, and those who remember it maintain that it was in all artistic requirements superior to the more commodious building by which it has been replaced.* The success of the design is the more surprising, as the College received from the architect only a general scheme which they carried out piecemeal, contracting for small portions of the work with different master-masons. Two of these contracts are preserved in the Register. The first, dated 1521, is with William Eist, mason, of Burford, for the making of certain windows; he is to have for his trouble £18, of which £10 are paid in advance. The other is with John Lobbens, mason, and William Jonson, freemason, for carving the lights

* A view of the old Chapel will be found in Ingram, *Memorials* (*Balliol*, p. 16). It was a buttressed building, half covered by ivy and creepers, with a low-pitched roof, and a belfry at the north-west corner.

of the east and other windows with "wovsers and chawmcrantes" and similar heraldic beasts; the price agreed upon was 21¼ marks. Altogether the Chapel must have been a heavy drain upon the resources of the College. But, as usual, benefactors were not wanting. Perhaps one of the most considerable was the venerable Mr. Robert Ascham to whom in 1523, on account of "his most munificent gifts," the Master and Fellows accorded

"free use of a tower situated over the College gates, containing two rooms, an upper and a lower, in such manner that he shall not in his absence assign the use of the said tower to any one . . . except with the consent of the Master and Fellows."

Mr. Robert Ascham may have been a member of the College, but the transaction was something more than a mere allotment of rooms, which might have been made by the Master on his sole responsibility. When we remember the smallness of the accommodation to be found in the College buildings at that time, it is obvious that the number of inmates must have been very small to admit of such a concession. The precise form which was taken by the liberality of Mr. Ascham cannot be ascertained; and our only detailed information concerning the benefactions to the Chapel is derived from the windows as described by Antony Wood. Of these there were eight in all, including the east window; four were on the north side, and three on the south. Among those who gave them are mentioned Thomas Leson, Dr. Hygdon, the first Dean of Cardinal College and sometime President of Magdalen, and Sir William Compton with his wife. Two of the windows were destroyed at some time in the sixteenth century, probably as "smelling of Popery and Superstition"; they were restored in 1636-37, when the College was under the influence of Laud, by the munificence of Richard Atkins, Esquire, Fellow-Commoner of the College, and Dr. Peter Wentworth, one of Strafford's kinsmen and a Fellow. The great east window, however, escaped the fury of the Edwardian Reformers. It represented "in lively Colours and exquisite Postures" the Passion, Resurrection and Ascension. Underneath, in the lower half of the window, was a portrait of the donor, Laurence Stubbs, a brother of the Master of that name and himself a President of Magdalen. This part of the window is still to be seen in the Undergraduates' Library. Laurence Stubbs is shown in a kneeling posture at a desk, and arrayed in his doctor's hood and gown. The two sections of the window were divided by an inscription: *Orate pro anima Magistri Laurentii Stubbs Sacrae Theologiae Professoris, et istius Collegii specialis Benefactoris, qui hanc fenestram procuravit sumptibus suis. Anno Domini* MDXXIX. So justly celebrated was this window that Nicholas Wadham offered to buy it for his own College at the price of £200. Another on the south side was contributed by the same Laurence, conjointly with his brother Richard. This, like the east window, was in two halves, an upper and lower, only here there were the portraits of two donors kneeling at two separate desks.

One more feature of the Chapel calls for remark. This was the little wing adjoining the Chancel and projecting into the front quadrangle. It contained two rooms, an upper and lower; the one was used in later times as an infirmary, but at first as a Fellow's chamber; in the other the muniments were stored and College meetings occasionally held. Known as "the treasury," this wing finds mention on more than one occasion in the annals of later times; but it was swept away with the main building to which it belonged, and the archives are now stored in the Bursary, opposite the Undergraduates' Library.

For some few years after the completion of the Chapel masses were regularly said for Laurence Stubbs, Robert Ascham, and the rest of those whose purses had been placed at the service of the College. But the time was fast approaching when this and many other ancient uses would be rudely abolished. The first rumble of the storm was heard in the very year, 1529, when the Chapel was on the point of being opened. Henry VIII. sent down to Oxford a certain Dr. John Bell, who had been at one time a member of Balliol, to sound the University on the question of the divorce, and to give Convocation "a right understanding" of the issues at stake. Even in his own College Bell was not likely to meet with a cordial reception when he came on such an errand. Supported by the Heads of Houses, he found the juniors staunch to the cause of the injured Queen, and several doctors of divinity spoke in no uncertain manner against the King's design. Events, however, were not to be controlled by the wishes of the University. The King had the support of Parliament, and when next he sent Commissioners to the University they came no longer to consult but to command. In 1534 all the Fellows of Colleges were required to take an oath acknowledging the Royal Supremacy. No evasion was possible, and most signed without protest. Only Balliol, where the Fellows were orthodox to the last degree and the Master was a nominee of Wolsey's own, ventured to qualify the submission. They would obey the King so far as they might without prejudice to divine law and the orthodox faith. The reservation was not unreasonable; but what courage was needed to say even thus much may be seen from the fact that Balliol stood utterly alone. All other corporations of whose conduct we know anything submitted absolutely, to the number of 167.*

So far the Colleges had escaped lightly. In the next year (1535) they were more roughly handled. Dr. London, the Warden of New College, and Layton, the future spoiler of the monasteries, made a visitation with the object of destroying all memorials of the Papal supremacy, "whether it were by pictures in glass windows or on signposts, or whether by name in printed or written service-books or parchments." So far as Balliol was concerned the only visible effect of their visit was to produce some erasures in the Register and the documents of the archives. The service-books appear, in part at least, to have escaped mutilation until the reign of Elizabeth. And two years later, in 1537, it was necessary for the Visitors to demand from the Fellows the surrender of five Papal Bulls, that the alterations required might be made in them. In 1536 the recognition of the Royal Supremacy was again demanded, in accordance with the Parliamentary Statute

---

* See the list in Rymer, *Foedera*, xiv. pp. 495-527. A copy of the Balliol submission is in the archives: the original is to be found in the Chapter House at Westminster.

of that year. This time there was no protestation. The College was cowed into submission.

Its members had no affection for Protestant principles. Whyte, the Master, grumbled as much as he dared, and if it had not been for his personal unpopularity he would easily have formed a party of reaction among the Fellows. Of all their number there appears to have been but one who was prepared to follow implicitly the lead of Cromwell. This was a certain George Cootes, of whom we shall have more to say. His sincerity may be judged from his later career. He held the Bishopric of Chester during the Marian persecutions, and the unction with which he defended the most vulnerable doctrines of the old faith drew, at that time, large crowds to his London pulpit.* The sentiments of his Balliol colleagues are shown by a casual entry in the Register (October 1538):

"Granted under our common seal to the Venerable Lady Anna Danvers that the Office for the Dead be said every year for the good of her soul and for her benefactions, on account of her gift of £30 to the Master and Fellows."

The Ten Articles forbade masses for the dead, but allowed prayers for their soul's health, and the College did not fail to keep as near the ancient usage as they might. †

The publication of the Six Articles served to show that the inrush of innovations was, for the time at all events, to be checked. Relieved from anxieties of more moment, the Fellows could now afford to indulge in a

---

* Machyn *Diary*, pp. 79, 165.

† Prayers for the Dead are to be found in the Prayer-book of 1549: but are altogether dropped from that of 1552. The Office for the Dead was read in Balliol Chapel at least as late as 1560.

wrangle over the Mastership. They were tired of William Whyte, as he of them. Only his heavy debts to the College prevented him from resigning, and retiring to spend his old age in a more congenial place. Here our friend George Cootes saw his opportunity. He suggested to the Master that a resignation in his favour would be acceptable to the College, and would be followed by a lenient composition for all outstanding debts. At the same time he intimated to the Fellows that his own election to the Mastership was the one condition upon which Whyte would resign. The coldness between Master and Fellows was such, that a little ingenuity served to prevent them from making the explanations which would have unmasked the deceit. The Fellows, "calling to mind how unkind a parent old Master Whyte had been," agreed to elect Cootes, although they had but a poor opinion of him, and applied to the formidable Vicar-General of the realm for leave to do so. In his capacity of Visitor the Bishop of Lincoln attempted to enlighten Cromwell as to the true character of their candidate.

"If Cootes should obtain Balliol," he wrote, "the College is undone. The man is so wilful and factious that there would soon be few in the College save of his own country [*sc.* Yorkshire]."

Cromwell hesitated and made inquiries among the Protestants of the University. Their opinion of Cootes was far more appreciative than the Bishop's.

"His judgment in Scripture," said one unsuspicious correspondent, "is well amended, and not addict to man's doctrine nor schoolmen's fantasies, but only to God's word. He takes much pains here in reading and preaching."

This was quite enough for Cromwell, who had more serious troubles on his hands. He wrung from the Bishop of Lincoln a reluctant assent to Cootes' appointment, after reminding him that the man might be put out of office if at any time he trangressed the ordinances of the College ; and the way being now clear he penned the following letter to the Fellows : *

"After my hearty commendations ; whereas by my last letter addressed to you I gave you commandment in the King's Majesty's name, that forthwith upon the receipt thereof, without any further citations delays or like solemnities of the law and notwithstanding the absence of any of your company, so that the more part were present, you should proceed to the election of a convenient master of your house there vacant, and that of your election so being made without any partiality or corruption you should incontinent certify me, to the end the same might be ratified as should appertain ; and forasmuch as according to the tenor and effect of the same you have assembled yourselves together, [and] upon good deliberation and advice taken therein have elected and chosen my friend Doctor Cott (sic), like as by your presentation sealed with your common seal I am ascertained; This shall be to signify unto you and every of you that I have perused and examined the same and every circumstance thereof, and do commend and allow your good proceedings therein, and have confirmed, ratified, and approved your said election, by

---

* This letter has been already printed from the Register by the Baroness de Paravicini. Our own text is taken from a contemporary copy in the Archives.

the authority committed unto me by the King's Highness in that behalf, willing and commanding you by these presents that you and every of you shall from henceforth repute, accept, and take the said Doctor Cott as the very rightful and just master of your House, using yourselves toward him in every condition with such duty and obedience as to the said office doth appertain, as you and every of you tender the King's Highness' pleasure. Thus fare you heartily well. From London, the 20th day of November [1539]. Your loving friend Thomas Crumwell."

Great was the disgust of the electors when they afterwards discovered the trick which had been played upon them, and each man realised that he had thrown away his own chances to avert an imaginary danger. They wrote to Cromwell stating the facts, and asked that they might make a new election. He replied by giving them permission to elect William Wryght, a popular Fellow five years junior in standing to Cootes. But the latter, helped no doubt by Cromwell's fall in June 1540, contrived to hold his own for some time. Five years elapsed before Wryght succeeded to the post for which Cromwell had singled him out. As may be imagined, these years were not the most peaceful period in the history of the College. The brief notices of the Register (now kept regularly by a secretary, appointed from among the Fellows at a salary of 6s. 8d.) enable us to picture a series of small quarrels which wrecked the harmony of the Fellows and injured discipline. At a meeting in the Chapel in 1543, the Master, having heard of some rumours unfriendly to himself, "interrogated the Fellows, whether any of them would assert that he, the said Master, had laboured for the election of a Fellow of the county of York." No one was bold enough to take up the glove. But two months later there was another angry scene in the same place, when Dr. Cootes "showed Mr. Howell a mandate bidding him conduct himself obediently and peaceably towards him and the Fellows, according to the tenor of the Statute." Mr. Howell appears to have been a *Scholasticus*. He was not the only one who showed himself wanting in respect for the unpopular Master. On November 7, 1543, Mr. Smythe was detected in the act of taking for his breakfast the commons which had been laid out in Hall for the Master's consumption. The injured dignity of Dr. Cootes required that the offender should be brought before a solemn conclave, consisting of himself, the offender's Tutor, and a Bursar. Fortunately for Mr. Smythe, the assessors took a lenient view of the offence, and he escaped with the loss of a week's commons.

In 1545 Cootes left the House, rather opportunely, as Protestantism no longer found favour in high places. While he was changing his convictions in some other climate, the College was quietly ruled by William Wryght, whose opinions, like those of most of the Fellows, were of the shade affected by the Norfolk party, then predominant at Court. But the day of Norfolk's fall soon arrived, and no sooner had Somerset assumed the protectorate than Wryght quietly slipped out of office. His place was taken by a man who might have been Cootes' twin brother, so close was the resemblance of their characters and fortunes. James Brookes was from the first a Romanist at heart, like most of the other Heads of colleges. He had the dexterity to avoid censure during the brief reign of Edward VI. At Mary's accession he showed himself in his true colours and was instantly rewarded by the Bishopric of Gloucester. He was consecrated in 1554, as one of a batch of six new prelates, hastily nominated to fill the places of the reformers; but he retained the Mastership until the following year, when the honest Wryght came back again to take up that position for the second time.

The memory of Brookes has not been spared either by his contemporary, Bishop Jewel, or by Fox the martyrologist. The former calls him "a beast of impure life and most impure conscience." The latter records with satisfaction how, when Brookes sat in judgment upon Cranmer and Latimer, the one taunted him with perjury, and the other confuted him out of his own writings. Still, in justice to Brookes it must be observed that his shifts and changes of opinion were not greater than the moral standard of the time permitted. He had never been blatant, like Cootes, in his hypocrisy. Nor does his conduct during the Marian era justify all the epithets which his accusers found for him. His behaviour to Cranmer and Latimer was marked by none of that savage brutality too often affected in such trials. In his own diocese he showed a bluff reluctance to go further in persecution than the exigencies of his position required. The apology of Antony Wood, though coming from a tainted source, ought not to be forgotten.

" As for Brookes he was a man of literature not vulgar, for eloquence not to be contemned, for his manner and courtesy to be beloved and respected, though much changed and perhaps weakened as to his religion by the variety of those times."

The statement that he died in agonies of remorse may be taken at its true worth, as a polemical flourish. He died in 1558 before there was anything to be gained by repentance.

Through a singular coincidence the burning of Cranmer and Latimer, which was the most important event of his life, is connected by local association with the name of his old College. Every visitor to Oxford is familiar with the Martyrs' Memorial which stands outside the back gate of Balliol of to-day. Though it does not mark the exact spot of the execution, it is near enough to satisfy all but the most exacting antiquarians. The Martyrs were burned "over against Balliol College" (which did not then extend so far as the Memorial), not far from the North Gate above which Bocardo prison was built, and in immediate proximity to the Canditch which laved the city wall at this point. This description points us to Broad Street, and in fact, some years ago, excavations revealed there a pile of ashes, charred wood, and fragments of human bones. A cross has been carved upon the Master's Lodgings exactly opposite the place where the gruesome discovery was made. There can be no reasonable doubt that those who wish to honour the memory of Cranmer and Latimer should make their pilgrimage to this cross.

No one in Balliol was likely to court martyrdom or even expulsion. The few scruples which remained over from the days of Thomas Cromwell were scattered to the winds by the eloquence of the Spanish friars, whom

From a photograph by the] *[Oxford Camera Club*
BACK GATE AND MARTYRS' MEMORIAL

Mary introduced into Oxford to disseminate sound doctrine. Balliol in fact became Catholic to the core, so that many years of Elizabeth's vigilant *régime* barely sufficed to make the College Anglican again.

During the years 1547–1566 the Library was the part of the College which suffered most. Needless to say that the Edwardian reformers were responsible for the damage. They came in 1553 and took away no small number of Gray's MSS., to be burned with ignominy in the market-place. From reproaches of this kind the Catholics were free. It is indeed recorded of the famous Jesuit, Parsons, that, when he was Bursar to the College, he sold many precious volumes. But history must do his communion the justice of adding that in those days he was a Calvinist of the deepest dye; and that the money which he received for the manuscripts was spent in purchasing some of that excellent Protestant divinity which now adorns the Library shelves.

The whips of Elizabeth touched the College more nearly than the scorpions of Mary. William Wryght, as might have been expected from his past career, refused to adopt the new settlement and retired from the Mastership. Francis Babington, a Fellow of All Souls, was invited to come and succeed him; nor was his the only new face which made its appearance in the little band of Fellows. Three retired in the same year as William Wryght; another followed them in 1560. Apparently their successors did not find themselves particularly welcome. A Mr. Barker, who was admitted as a chaplain in August 1559, threw up his Fellowship before a year was out. Babington too accepted the Rectorship of Lincoln and so departed. Others, however, refused to retire from the battle; among them we notice the not too respectable Adam Squier, who afterwards rose to rule the fortunes of the College.*

With the accession of Elizabeth begins a new era in the history of Balliol. It had been Catholic, it was about to be Puritan. The theological nature of the foundation made it almost impossible for the body of the Fellows to pursue a middle course. They had trained a Brookes in this age, in the next they were to train an Abbott. But, before we turn to follow the course of the new development, an apology is due for a chapter which has almost ignored the undergraduate. He was not a common phenomenon at Balliol in the first half of the sixteenth century. A census of the Colleges, taken in 1552,† enumerates twenty-nine residents at Balliol. Of these eight were Masters of Arts, six were Bachelors, and four were matriculated servants. This leaves but eleven undergraduates, of whom the majority would be scholars.‡ Bishop Fox had impressed upon the foundation a character which did not attract the average parent. The study of the classics had been checked, and the atmosphere must have been overpoweringly clerical. We have already commented on the significance of the privilege accorded to Robert Ascham. The precedent was followed more than once.

* Wood *MSS*. F. 28, fol. 54. A list of Fellows of Balliol with dates, compiled from the Register.

† Boase, *Register* (Oxf. Hist. Soc.).

‡ The largest College in 1552 was Christ Church, which contained one hundred and thirty-one matriculated Members. There were thirteen Colleges and eight Halls. St. Edmund's Hall, the smallest of the whole list, contained nine Members. Of the Colleges, Oriel and University were smaller than Balliol, Lincoln exactly the same size.

A deed in the archives tells how, in 1551, the College leased a set of rooms to an outsider, John Howe. An entry in the Register of somewhat later date (1557) records that Mr. Antony Garnett, having decorated and adorned a large room near the Library at his own expense, was authorised to retain the said room for the term of four years after the expiration of his Fellowship. There were no juniors waiting to have lodgings allotted to them. Even those who were on the books showed no desire to come within the walls. In 1561 the College decreed "that no Commoner be permitted to lodge in the City or suburbs for a whole week, month or term unless for an urgent, good, and legitimate cause . . . if he desire to make any use of our College."

What Commoners there were at this time appear to have come chiefly from Wales and the Welsh marches. The Tudors, in their zeal for the civilisation of the Principality of which they were natives, encouraged the influx of Welshmen into Oxford, and as until 1571 there was no College specially provided for them, they found their way into most of those already existing. According to Antony Wood their character was not of the most peaceful, and in the brawls of the sixteenth century they won the same prominence as the Irish students, or "chamberdekyns," in the fourteenth and fifteenth. The Library contains one curious memorial of the Welsh immigration, in the shape of a commonplace book, commenced by John Price, one of the familiars of Thomas Cromwell, and containing a collection of Welsh songs and ballads.

The junior element in the College received a slight and not very desirable augmentation under the will of

Dr. John Bell, sometime Bishop of Worcester. Having resigned his See from religious scruples, Bell lived quietly until his death in a house at Clerkenwell which had been, before 1539, the abode of Benedictine nuns. This house he bequeathed to the College on condition that it should found two exhibitions for Worcestershire men *in grammatica expertis*. The legacy caused the College trouble in more ways than one. By accepting it without a licence from the Crown the Master and Fellows laid themselves open to the penalties of the Statute of Mortmain. Some one informed against them in the Court of Chancery, and they were fain to purchase a pardon from Philip and Mary. Even then their title could not be considered a good one, for while a Catholic ruled in England, there was always the remote contingency of the resumption of the monastic lands. They had therefore to procure from the aged prioress, to whose community the house in question had once belonged, a renunciation of all her rights. At length, in 1558, the title was secured, and two exhibitions were founded, each of £20, tenable for four years. They were the first of those local charities which now began to be tacked upon the old foundation, and which did so much to ruin its credit. Local exhibitions are only to be tolerated when the institution to which they belong is a large one, when the area from which their holders are drawn is wide, and when they are awarded with strict regard to merit. Otherwise they inevitably become gifts in the hands of careless patrons; they infuse a parochial spirit into a College; and they lower it in the estimation of the outside world. In our own century University Commissions have removed the more pernicious restrictions to which endowments of this kind had been subjected by the caprice of short-sighted testators. Balliol, furthermore, has had the courage on more than one recent occasion to reject the offer of close scholarships, when their rules appeared inconsistent with the spirit of the place. Two centuries ago the Master and Fellows failed to pursue this obviously sound policy; the consequences of their neglect will be more fully noted in succeeding chapters.

Some curious light is thrown upon the social life of the College by a custumal appended to the Register about this date. It relates almost entirely to Gaudies and Feasts. On Saturday night, after the usual disputations in Hall, the Fellows are allowed

"so much bread to their supper as they will eat, leaving also to the scholars or servitors bread according to the discretion of the master or senior which may be present; the fellows may choose whether they will be allowed their bread or drink, but commonly they have taken their bread, both because the scholars might have part allowance thereby, and for other causes."

On Easter Eve, and also in Rogation Week, "in consideration that it is a Gaudy Week, and for that then there is but one meal a day," the Fellows are allowed to spend what they like, in reason, upon their dinners. On St. Thomas Day the Bursar gives an audit dinner. At Easter, Christmas, Whitsuntide, and on St. Catharine's day, the Master and Fellows are allowed a breakfast in the morning, "with stewed meat or such other." On Midsummer Day and some other occasions they "were wont to have an hour's drinking, with cakes and fine ale." Such festivities concluded with the singing of an hymn or anthem. It was all the more necessary to insist upon them as the High Table was the only place where the seniors of the community habitually foregathered for social intercourse. Common rooms were not yet in fashion; and the ordinary meal in Hall appears to have been a cheerless performance, evaded when possible, and hurried over with indecent speed. Special legislation was necessary to prevent the Fellows from carrying away their commons to be consumed in the solitude of their own rooms.

CHAPTER VI

JESUIT AND PURITAN, 1559-1603

Masters: Francis Babington, 1559; Antony Garnet, 1560; Richard Hooper, 1563; Robert Hooper, 1567; John Piers, 1570; Adam Squier, 1571; Edmund Lilly, 1580.

During the reign of Elizabeth the University gained in popularity as a place of education for young men of means. Balliol shared with other colleges in the return of prosperity, and for the second time in her history became full of Commoners. Bishop Fox in his Statutes had provided for the reception of such inmates; and in the absence of information from Bursar's Books and other documents of the kind we are unable to assert that there had been no Commoners at all in the College during the first half of the century. If, however, there were many Commoners between 1507 and 1544 they did not distinguish themselves in any way, neither had the College taken the most elementary and essential steps to provide a system of tuition for them. After 1544 this state of things was gradually altered. The studies and the conduct of the Commoners were placed under careful supervision. Education became the chief duty of the Fellows, who, although at variance on many burning questions of the day, were at least agreed as to the necessity of adapting the College to the new requirements of the age.

The first intimation of the change is to be found in the decree of 1571, which provides that every Commoner on admission shall find some approved surety for the payment of his debts to the College; and that, while each Fellow is to be held responsible for the solvency of his Scholar, the Bursars shall answer to the College for the battells of the Commoners, and, in consideration of this liability, shall be entitled to take for themselves whatever profit is made by the sale of bread, beer, and other eatables to the said Commoners. The natural inference seems to be that a section of the Fellows regarded the Commoner with some suspicion, as a possibly expensive novelty, and that the College was in fear of suffering pecuniary loss through ill-advised admissions. The University census of 1572 enables us to say, with some exactness, what proportion the new element bore to the old. The number of residents has more than doubled. There are now sixty-five inmates, of whom forty-six are undergraduates. In the second of these totals are included eight Scholars and nine Servitors or matriculated servants, which leaves us with twenty-nine Commoners. Half a century afterwards the number of Commoners had risen from twenty-nine to seventy, a figure which is surpassed by Exeter alone among the remaining Colleges. In 1612 Exeter had no less than a hundred and thirty-four Commoners; but this exceptional prosperity arose in part at least from the successful management of Dr. Thomas Holland, who had been for some years a Fellow and Tutor of Balliol. For the period intervening between 1572 and 1612 the matriculation tables of the University give some assistance, although they are undoubtedly defective. Between 1574 and 1596 the names of three hundred and twenty-six persons are recorded as matriculating from Balliol. This gives us an annual average of fourteen or fifteen. The greatest number matriculating in any single year of this period is forty-two (1581); but this is a quite exceptional figure, and to be explained by the fact that, owing to the Jesuit invasion, great efforts were being made to procure an accurate list of undergraduates, and to drive all of them into some college or hall. Among the forty-two matriculants were undoubtedly some persons who had entered the College in the three years immediately preceding, but had omitted to inscribe their names upon the University books. A curious feature of these lists is a sudden shrinkage which occurs as soon as the war with Spain becomes imminent. In 1586 and 1587 there were only nine matriculants. In 1588, when the peril of the Armada had passed away, the number of entries suddenly mounts to eleven, and for the next eight years the average is perfectly normal.

These figures would lead us to believe that the sea was for a time a rival of the University. That supposition is confirmed by the careers of two Balliol men who flourished at this time. In 1579 Lawrence Kemyss entered the College as a Scholar; in 1582 he was elected to a Fellowship on account of his proficiency in the mathematical sciences. But either he discovered that the demand for mathematical tutors was slight, or else his adventurous soul grew weary of the interminable theological debates of his colleagues.

In 1589, at the mature age of twenty-eight, he threw up his Fellowship and enlisted in the service of Sir Walter Raleigh, whose society he doubtless found much more congenial than that of George Abbott the Puritan, then the leading spirit in Balliol. Kemyss it was who came to Raleigh in his imprisonment in the Tower, bringing the lump of gold-quartz and the traveller's tales of gold mines on the Orinoco which lured the great adventurer to his doom. How Kemyss mismanaged the expedition which he had prompted, and how he took his own life to escape the reproaches of his unhappy master, are stories familiar to all who have the least acquaintance with the events of Raleigh's last voyage. Less well known, but more fortunate, was Edmund Monson, who entered Balliol as a Commoner two years later than Kemyss. Learning of any kind was little to his taste, "his mind being more martial than mercurial." In 1583 he was off to sea, without having taken a degree or even kept his terms. But his merits as a sailor were soon recognised. He served with distinction in several expeditions against the Spaniards, was knighted by the Earl of Essex at the sack of Cadiz in 1596, and became first Vice-Admiral, then Admiral of the Narrow Seas.

No doubt the College would have produced more navigators if it had drawn more largely upon Devon and the other maritime counties. But, until 1588, Wales, Worcestershire, Staffordshire, and Shropshire supplied the larger proportion of her Commoners. It is only at the end of the century that we begin to remark an influx from London and the counties south of the Thames. Those Balliol men who belonged to families of local reputation turned to the studies which befitted the future rulers of inland districts. When they left the College it was usually to enter their names at one of the Inns of Court, where they might learn law enough to become the Silents and Shallows of their own neighbourhood. Some, however, carried their studies deeper, and found the Bar so attractive as to make it their profession. No less than four distinguished judges of this period came from Balliol. Sir Thomas Coventry (1547-1606), Justice of the Common Pleas, is mentioned as a Probationer-Fellow in 1565. His son Thomas, Lord Coventry (1578-1640), was a Commoner who left the College without taking a degree; this premature departure was, however, due to no want of ability; for he afterwards became Attorney-General to James I., and Lord Keeper to Charles I. Equally short was the residence of Sir Humphrey Davenport (1566-1645), who figures in history, first as Counsel for the Crown against Eliot and Selden (1629), afterwards as the first of those judges whom Charles I. was ill-advised enough to appoint *durante beneplacito*, and not for life or good behaviour (1630). That these men were intimately connected with the College, or that their debt to it was considerable, cannot safely be assumed. But the fact that they belonged to Balliol seems to prove the reputation of the tutors whom the College produced at this time. There is yet another lawyer of whom we must speak. Sir John Popham (1531-1607), though never a Fellow, is of some importance in the constitutional history of Balliol; for he took pains, in his capacity of executor to Mr. Peter Blundell, to make his old College the recipient of that excellent clothier's bounty. Little else can be said in his favour. Of unprepossessing appearance, "a huge, heavy, ugly man," he was still more unfortunate in the reputation which, deservedly or not, he acquired among his contemporaries. As a young barrister he is said to have taken purses on Shooter's Hill. As a judge he had the misfortune to be concerned in two notorious trials which cast a grave shadow of suspicion upon the bench. He tried the notorious Dayrell of Littlecote for the murder of his infant child; by a strange coincidence Dayrell was acquitted, but the manor of Littlecote, with the curse attaching to it, came into Popham's possession. There is stronger evidence for censuring his conduct, as Chief Justice, at the trial of Sir Walter Raleigh (1603-4). He kept, indeed, within the letter of the law, which is more than can be said for some of his contemporaries on the bench; and he appears to have been firmly convinced of the prisoner's guilt; but these facts can hardly excuse the animus which he ostentatiously displayed.

In spite of the increased numbers, the domestic arrangements of the College in this period retained their primitive simplicity. The staff of servants was small. The Bursars' Books make mention of ten only, one of whom was specially attached to the person of the Master. A cook, an under cook, a manciple, and a butler performed all those necessary indoor services which were not put upon the poorer members of the foundations. The servants' duties were lightened by the fact that Balliol, unlike some other colleges, neither brewed nor baked. Bread and beer were regularly supplied by tradespeople of the town. On the other hand, the staff included a barber, a washerwoman, a carpenter, and a tiler, all of whom were regularly employed but found lodgings in the town. There was also a gardener, from which we infer that the Fellows and Scholars had ceased to grow their own cabbages and posies. Perhaps the ornamental garden, which is so conspicuous in later prints of the College, had already come into existence.

It was well that the domestic arrangements were simple, for they were sometimes subjected to a violent dislocation. Once or twice the College was compelled to migrate from Oxford, owing to a severe visitation of the plague. In 1563 every one except the Senior Bursar retired to the village of Church Handborough near Woodstock; the devoted Bursar remained to keep up the Chapel services, and to look after the disinfection of the rooms. In 1571 these half measures were regarded as insufficient. The Master and Fellows decreed that every one might go whither he would until the epidemic had abated. The College was closed in May and did not reassemble until the following February.

Fortunately these little accidents did not permanently affect the popularity of the College. Commoners continued to flow in; the Master and Fellows were continually engaged in making new arrangements for their accommodation. In 1587 it was decreed that every Commoner must have a Tutor, must perform the same exercises and disputations as the Scholars, and must show the same reverence to the Master and Fellows. They were forbidden to indulge in the bad habit of dining in their own rooms; all commons were ordered to be served and eaten in Hall. No one was allowed to go into the kitchen or the buttery at meal-times, except the Fellows and the servants duly appointed for that purpose. The College was now so far from suspecting the Commoners of insolvency, that the Bursars were relieved from their former liability for battells; but at the same time it was decreed that all battells must be paid within a fortnight of the end of term. The room-rents made so considerable a difference in the revenues, that it was now found possible to increase the commons of Fellows to five shillings, and those of Scholars to tenpence a week. The Fellows, it will be seen, took the lion's share of the new profits. It was an unfair arrangement, for they made money out of the Commoners in their individual capacity. The tutorial system was totally different from that which now prevails. A parent on bringing up his son made his own choice of a tutor; the tutor undertook to look after the finances, the conduct, and the reading of his pupil, and stood to him *in loco parentis;* the fees were a matter of private agreement. From the outside point of view, the College was little more than a society of "coaches," who lived and compelled their charges to live under one common roof.* A minor result of the system, which is not without its bearing on the fortunes of the College, was that Fellows with a large connection were relatively independent of the Master and their colleagues; for they could always meet a threat of punishment for breaches of discipline with the counter-threat that they would carry off their *clientèle.*

---

* There was a scheme of College lectures. Three Praelectors were annually appointed in the subjects of Latin, Greek, and Theology. They do not, however, seem to have been satisfactory teachers.

It is hard to give an accurate idea of the financial position from the Bursars' Books. The accounts were made up half-yearly, in July and at Luke-tide, and a fairly continuous series of these statements beginning with 1578 is still to be seen. But owing to the system of beneficial leases the revenue fluctuated considerably from year to year. In some half-years the *Recepta* fall below the sum of £30; in others they will be considerably more than £100. But before the year 1580 the average revenue seems to be something under £150, and after that date something under £200. When the Queen visited Oxford the College was assessed for the purposes of her entertainment as having a revenue of £100. It is worthy of notice that the political troubles of the last two reigns do not seem to have seriously affected the value of the Balliol estates. Under Elizabeth the expenditure increased almost as rapidly as the revenue, so that the surplus was very little larger at the end of the century than it had been in the middle. What increase there was partly went to augment the commons and allocations of the Fellows; doubtless the remainder was divided according to the practice then first coming into vogue. For it is certain that the College could not, or would not, spend any considerable sum out of the treasury on the alterations and extensions of the buildings which were so much needed. The one great addition to the fabric, that of Hammond's buildings, was due to the liberality of an individual fellow, Mr. William Hammond, who gave, in 1594, £1000 for this purpose. Hammond's lodgings were erected on the south side of the back quadrangle, west of the Master's House, and facing Broad Street. They occupied the site of old Balliol Hall, the original domicile of John de Balliol's scholars, which the College had acquired in the reign of Edward III. Hammond's lodgings stood by themselves. On the side of the quadrangle facing St. Mary Magdalen there were only a few tenements, such as the hostelry of the Catharine Wheel, which had been leased to townspeople. It is unfortunate that we have no further information concerning the benefactor by whom the building of the back quadrangle was thus commenced. One of his autograph letters may be seen in the archives, but it is a purely formal request for a power of attorney, and tells nothing of interest respecting himself or the Master and Fellows to whom it was addressed.

We have now passed in review the chief facts bearing upon the undergraduate life of the College in the reign of Elizabeth. But within the narrow circle of the Fellows events were passing of little interest. Here were to be found all the necessary conditions for a series of dramatic quarrels. The expulsions of 1559 and 1560 had failed, in Balliol more than in most Colleges, to produce a harmony of opinion on religious questions. Among the genuine conformers there were two parties, of which the more extreme desired still further reforms in the direction of Calvinism. Some of those who, by a judicious dissimulation, had saved their places for the present, were far from acquiescing in the religious settlement of Henry VIII. and Elizabeth; the Court, while sticking at no degree of unlawful pressure to secure the appointment of desirable candidates, had shown little discretion in its patronage.

The appointment of Babington to the Mastership

will serve as an illustration. During the Marian persecutions he had been prominent in the University as a supporter of the reaction, and there is no reason to believe that his conformity at Elizabeth's accession was in the least sincere. But he had made interest with the Earl of Leicester, whose chaplain he had become. It was, doubtless, the powerful favourite who put him into Balliol, as afterwards into Lincoln. The hypocrisy of Babington might long have remained unsuspected, but for a piece of rashness which does some credit to his heart, and casts a black suspicion on his master. Babington was called upon in 1560 to preach the funeral sermon of Amy Robsart, and in doing so spoke of her as "pitifully murdered." Leicester was a dangerous man to accuse. In 1569 Babington found it expedient to leave the country. His record was subjected to a searching examination, and in 1565, a year after the appointment of Leicester as Chancellor of the University, he was publicly proclaimed a Romanist, and all his benefices were declared forfeit. It was less easy to destroy the traces of his influence. For some years afterwards Lincoln remained, in the words of Mr. Clark, a Romanist seminary. Balliol, in a less degree, shared the reproach. The Visitor in 1565 found it necessary to issue the following ordinances :

(1) That all inmates of the House shall take the Lord's Supper "according to the order set forth in the Book of Common Prayer" at least three or four times in the year.

(2) They shall be regular in their attendance at the usual chapel-services; these services to be in the vulgar tongue; any one failing to attend shall be "punished with

stripes if he be under correction, or else have one farthing set upon his head."

(3) That all Latin primers, not allowed by the Queen's majesty, and all other superstitious books . . . be brought to the Master and forthwith demolished.

(4) That the Master bring with him all his company to the University sermons.

Two years later the brother of the famous Henry Garnett (still a Scholar at Winchester) was expelled from his Fellowship; although the cause is not stated, we can hardly account for it otherwise than on religious grounds. Thomas Garnett had been brought up as a Protestant; but within a few years from this date, he, his brother, his mother, and his sister were all pronounced Romanists.

A more serious struggle followed. The younger Fellows were profoundly moved by the religious struggles of the time. They devoured the controversial literature of the times, and as the natural result drifted on the one hand or the other far from the *Via Media* which the practical statesmanship of the Queen had devised. Hence arose a feud in the College, which was complicated partly by personal animosities, still more by the sudden and violent revulsions of conviction which some experienced, as new arguments suddenly dawned upon their minds. The college career of Robert Parsons is the best commentary upon the situation. In the account which follows we have combined, as far as possible, the narrative of Parsons' younger brother, who was an undergraduate at the time,[*] with the informa-

[*] *Records of the English Province* (ed. Foley), vi. p. 679.

tion given in the Lives by Dr. James (1612)* and Anthony Wood, and with the reminiscences of Archbishop Abbott.

Robert Parsons was the "son of a plebeian of honest repute." He entered Balliol as a Scholar, in 1568 became a Probationer-Fellow, and shortly afterwards was appointed Chaplain and Bursar. As a tutor he was extremely successful; his connections in London and the west-country had the effect of gathering round him the largest band of pupils in the College. But his religious opinions were unsettled; both his friends and his enemies notice that not a few of his pupils afterwards followed him over to Rome. Though he had been bred a Calvinist, and continued in that persuasion for some years, there were family influences at work to drag him the other way. His father became a Catholic in 1563, and he himself, justly or not, was suspected while still a Fellow of leaning that way. His retirement, however, was precipitated by other causes. The Master, Adam Squier, was a stalwart Churchman much disposed to resent enthusiasm in any shape or form; and unfortunately for himself the enthusiasm of Parsons led him to satirise the Master's private life and conduct. Neither was Squier the only sufferer. According to Abbott, the future Jesuit "was a man at that time wonderfully given to scoffing, and that with bitterness, which also was the reason that none of the company loved him." Thus there was formed against him a cabal headed by one Christopher Bagshaw, who, being

* *The Jesuit's Downfall; with the Life of Father Parsons*, by Dr. James, Bodley's Librarian. There is a copy of this pamphlet in the Bodleian, and it appears to have been used by Wood.

himself a violent Puritan, hated Parsons for his supposed Romanist tendencies, was the more bitter because Parsons had "swinged" him for misbehaviour in his undergraduate days. Bagshaw and the Master raked up against their enemy a series of charges, any one of which would have justified his expulsion. They said that he was a Papist in disguise; then that as Bursar he had falsified the College accounts to his own advantage; finally that he was born out of lawful wedlock, and so incapable of holding a Fellowship under Fox's Statutes. In the end Parsons found himself compelled to resign.* Clearly his guilt was not proved to the satisfaction of all; for he received permission to retain his rooms and his pupils for a while. But his persecutors were not to be balked. They caused the bells of St. Mary Magdalen to be rung in honour of the event, and otherwise displayed their malicious exultation, until he was fairly hounded out of the College and the University, "with whouts and hobubs." He went to London (1574), and by the sale of his effects raised money enough to carry him to the University of Padua. According to his brother he was not a Catholic at the time, but only "minded to be." His last scruples were overcome during a stay which he made at Louvain on the outward journey. Rome, instead of Padua, became his destination; in 1575 he entered the Society of Jesus as a novice. He was destined to revisit Oxford once more, but in far other than a Scholar's garb. He came over to England in 1580, on a mission from the Pope, disguised as a soldier "in a suit of buff laid with

---

* The entry in the Register ran "*sponte et coactus*"; but the "*et*" has been crossed out, and "*non*" written above.

gold lace"; and immediately set up a secret printing press, with which he roamed the country disseminating Romanist literature. On Commemoration Day, when all the University came to St. Mary's for the sermon, they found on every seat a copy of a tract by Campian, Parsons' fellow-Jesuit, the *Decem Rationes* in favour of the old religion. They had been printed by Parsons in a wood near Henley, but how he introduced them into the University Church remains an unsolved mystery.

The oddest feature of the whole story still remains to be mentioned. Christopher Bagshaw, not long after his rival's expulsion, passed over from Calvinism to Romanism, and fled the country to become a seminary priest. He was for some time an inmate of the English College at Rome, but his quarrelsome disposition caused his expulsion; he died a member of the Sorbonne. After his departure there was little to disturb the monotony of daily life in the College. The Masters who succeeded Babington were staunch Anglicans. Two of them, John Piers and Edmund Lilly, found favour in the eyes of Elizabeth for that reason. The former migrated from Balliol, after holding the Mastership for one year, to the Deanery at Christchurch (1571); thence to the See of Rochester (1576); thence to Salisbury (1589); and at length was created Archbishop of York. The fortunes of Edmund Lilly were less splendid. "He was Chaplain to Queen Elizabeth, and had been preferred by her, had not his long-winded sermon displeased her, when State-business occasioned her to enjoin him brevity." So he was left to lavish his eloquence in the narrow arena of College disputations.

"He was an excellent Divine, universally read in the Fathers, all whose opinions he would reckon up upon any question at Divinity Disputations in the College; and that with such volubility of Language and rivers of Eloquence, as made all covet to hear him, and his very Enemies to admire him."

Under his rule the College produced three Fellows of rather different views from his own and of far greater intellectual distinction. These were the two Abbotts, of whom more hereafter, and Dr. Thomas Holland. The last-named, after holding a Chaplain-Fellowship at Balliol, was made, in 1589, Regius Professor of Divinity. " He was an Apollos mighty in the Scriptures. He was familiarly conversant with the Fathers, and as a Father amongst them." In 1592 Queen Elizabeth's influence made him Rector of Exeter College; he was chosen for this post as a man well fitted for the task of subduing the Catholic leaven which had found its way into Exeter and showed no less vitality there than at Balliol. That Holland answered to the judgment which the Queen had formed of his character may be inferred from the anecdote which Savage tells of him. Whenever he started on a journey he used to quit his fellows with this valediction, " Commendo vos dilectioni Dei et odio Papatus et omnis superstitionis." Under his rule Exeter became the home of a moderate Puritan school, who, while hating ceremonies and vestments, remained faithful to the Church of England. Of Holland's later career we need only say that he was one of those whom James I. appointed to prepare the Authorised Version, and that with six other Oxford Scholars he made himself responsible for the translation of the prophets.

The benefactions made to the College in this period were not numerous. The most considerable, after that of Mr. Hammond, was Tony Foster's. The *ci-devant* custodian of Amy Robsart had a brother who was at one time a Fellow of the College; there is no other obvious reason for his legacy of £200 (1583). Doctor John Warner bequeathed in 1564 the sum of £20, with smaller gratuities for the Master, Fellows, and Scholars. It had now become usual for Fellows and Commoners to give some trifling present on their departure, though it was not the practice to levy a stated toll from them, as afterwards from the Fellow-Commoners. Thus, in 1557, John Smyth bequeathed six silver spoons, and Robert Crane, in 1583, gave a silver cup. The most curious souvenir of all was that presented by William Bell—a horn to summon the College to dinner. Queen's was the only other College which appears to have preferred the note of the horn to the more familiar dinner-bell; and in their case the usage had been prescribed by the Founder.

CHAPTER VII

PURITAN AND ANGLICAN—BLUNDELL'S TRUST

Masters: Edmund Lilly, 1580; Robert Abbott, 1609; John Parkhurst, 1616; Thomas Lawrence, 1637.

WE noted in our last chapter that Balliol had by the year 1612 attained to a certain prominence in University life. Unfortunately this prosperity rested on a very slender basis; and only exceptional ability amongst the teaching Fellows could counteract the deadening effect of extreme poverty. Poverty is not too strong a word; for an assessment taken in the year 1593, when the Colleges were required to contribute according to their means to the entertainment of Queen Elizabeth, shows Balliol in possession of corporate revenues amounting only to £100 a year, a figure which shows very poorly beside the £1000 of New College, the £1200 of Magdalen, and the £2000 of Christ Church.* An assessment of this kind must be regarded with caution, but it probably represents with substantial accuracy the relative wealth of the foundations named. It is more or less confirmed by the Laudian proctorial cycle of 1629. While Christ Church is allowed six proctors in

* The gross income was nearly double this amount (see *ante*, p. 103).

the ten years' period, Magdalen five, and New College four, Balliol has to be content with one only, and stands, along with University, Lincoln, Jesus, and Pembroke, in the lowest class of all. The great number of Commoners who resorted to Balliol at the commencement of the seventeenth century is only another proof of the pecuniary embarrassments which their presence did something to alleviate. With the exception of Magdalen and Exeter, none of the wealthy Colleges were anxious to burden themselves with ordinary educational work.

It is always dangerous to infer that, because a College produces eminent men, therefore it offers special advantages to the student. Davenport, Popham, and the two Coventries appear to have owed to Balliol little more than a lodging during their brief sojourn in Oxford.* But when we find that the College trained between 1589 and 1647 two Regius Professors of Divinity (Holland and Robert Abbott), a Margaret Professor (Dr. Lawrence), a Public Orator (Dr. Wenman), a Professor of Medicine (Thomas Clayton), an Archbishop, several Bishops and two or three distinguished Orientalists, we are perhaps justified in supposing that the Fellows of the day read and taught with more than usual industry.

In 1610 the Master and Fellows made a bold bid for popularity by providing for the admission of Fellow-Commoners, a class of students hitherto encouraged at two or three Colleges only (*e.g.*, Merton, C.C.C., and Magdalen.) The decree authorised the admission of "extraneos quoscumque quos appellant communarios" to the High Table. They were to attend chapel, and pursue the same course of studies as the Scholars, but

* *Supra*, p. 99.

were subject merely to lighter punishments. If they neglected their duties a Dean was to administer a reprimand in private; if this had no effect, they should be dealt with according to their age and the nature of the offence. Evelyn, who entered as a Fellow-Commoner in 1637, bears witness to the laudable impartiality with which these rules were enforced. "The Fellow-Commoners in Balliol were no more exempt from exercise than the meanest Scholars there." In return for his privileges each Fellow-Commoner was required to give £5 for the purchase of books or plate; but it appears that, after 1630, these sums were often appropriated to the Chapel, which needed many small repairs and additions to bring it up to the high standard of decency required by Laud.* The practice of admitting Fellow-Commoners almost died a natural death in the course of the Civil War and hardly revived until about the year 1670.

The College derived more credit from the admission of another exceptional class of inmates. These were Greeks, chiefly men of mature age, who came to Oxford for the purpose of pursuing theological and linguistic studies. Among Balliol men there were some who had travelled in the Levant, and were linguists "to whom great Avicenne might speak and be understood without an interpreter." Foreign Scholars were naturally attracted to such a society, and three at least are specially mentioned as having entered their names at Balliol, and resided there some little time. The first to arrive was one Christopher Angelus, a native of the Peloponnesus,

* In 1636 the College spent £328 on the Chapel. Of this sum £100, given by the son of Chief Justice Popham, was expended on a carved wooden screen, with St. Catharine standing on it. This figure is now in the Old Library.

whom the persecutions of the Turks had forced to quit his country. After dwelling for about three years in Trinity College, Cambridge, he migrated in 1610 to Balliol, which pleased him so much that he made it his home. He became celebrated as a teacher of Greek, and his popularity was much increased by the scars, which he would display as a proof of his sufferings to sympathetic auditors. Seven years later Archbishop Abbott sent to the College Metrophanes Critopylus, a Levantine priest, who had come over to qualify himself for preferment in the East. To him also a stay in Balliol appears to have been profitable, for soon after his departure in 1622 he became Patriarch of Alexandria. The third and the most described of these visitors was a Cretan, Nathaniel Conopius, who had been chaplain to Cyril, Patriarch of Constantinople, but was obliged to flee from that city in consequence of the murder of his patron. Conopius was well known to Savage and Evelyn, who were his contemporaries in College. The former tells us that "he (Conopius) spake and wrote the genuine Greek, which must be understood of prose, for the poetical Greek he had not. As for his writing, I have seen a great book of Music, as he said of his own composing"; but, remembering proverbs as to Cretan veracity, Dr. Savage declines to endorse this statement; neither will he vouch for the merits of the music, for "the notes were such as are not in use by any of the Western Churches." Evelyn remarks the curious fact that the practice of drinking coffee was introduced into Oxford by Conopius, who drank it every morning of his own making.*

* The first Oxford coffee-house was opened by Jacob, a Jew, about 1650, in a house between St. Edmund's Hall and Queen's College.

Though it had such interesting company to offer, Balliol rapidly waned in popularity and lost the reputation which had been acquired under the rule of Edmund Lilly. Theological controversy, which, in the early stages of the Reformation, had given a decided impetus to the pursuit of learning, was now, in the manner of Saturn, devouring her own children. The members of Balliol contributed more than their due share of heat to the discussions of the day. Until 1625, Balliol was one of the strongholds of that blatant Puritanism which vexed the soul of Laud during his residence at St. John's. At the beginning of the century George Abbott was the master-mind of this movement. After residing in Balliol, as Fellow and Tutor, for no less than fourteen years (1583–1597) he became the Master of University. His brother had retired from Balliol to a Worcestershire living in 1588; but when George Abbott became Primate, Robert reappeared on the scene, and as Regius Professor, naturally took up the attack upon the "Arminian" camp. We are told that he was more moderate than Dr. Holland, his predecessor in the Chair of Theology. If this be true, one can only sigh for some specimens of Holland's polemical eloquence, to show what Balliol men of the day considered a truly rousing sermon; for this degenerate age will find it hard to imagine how the following gem of Abbott's pulpit style could be surpassed in vigour. It is, we may remark, an apostrophe addressed to Laud from the University pulpit:

"Might not Christ say, what art thou? Romish or English, Papist or Protestant?—or what art thou? A mongrel compound of both; a Protestant by ordination, a

Papist in point of free will, inherent righteousness, and the like. A Protestant in receiving the Sacrament, a Papist in the doctrine of the Sacrament. What, do you think there be two heavens? if there be, get you to the other, and place yourself there, for into this where I am, ye shall not come."*

It must, in justice to Abbott, be added that he had other and more useful gifts than that of a biting tongue. Those who knew both the brothers said that, though the Archbishop was a more plausible preacher, "yet Robert was a greater scholar, and though an able statesman yet Robert was a deeper divine." Such as he was Robert Abbott received on Lilly's death the suffrages of the Balliol Fellows; and at Balliol he remained until 1616, when he was called away to the See of Sarum. His successor, John Parkhurst, was a bookworm of neutral opinions, whose natural inertia enabled him to satisfy without disquietude the requirements of two successive Primates so widely different in their views as Abbott and Laud. Under Parkhurst the discipline of the House fell to pieces. Those of the Fellows who had no taste for argument solaced themselves with good living, while the storm of words rattled over their heads. Archbishop Abbott still thought it worth his while to cultivate the friendship of Balliol. In 1616 he presented the Master and Fellows with the sum of £100. In 1619 he "expended divers sums" in repairing the Library and increasing the number of books. Again, in 1624, when an unluckly law-suit with Pembroke College had ended in total discomfiture, he paid out of

* Quoted by Mr. Hutton (Clarke, *Oxford Colleges*, p. 354).

his own pocket costs and damages amounting to £300. In a way he was rewarded; for his party found some recruits in Balliol between the years 1620 and 1630. But zeal outran the limits of discretion, and even of the Primate's wishes. He cannot have valued very highly the support of Mr. Tobias Crispe,* who transferred himself hither from Cambridge in 1624 or 1625, on account of difficulties, religious or otherwise, with unsympathetic College authorities. Crispe, who came with the character of a rigid Arminian, slid round by degrees to the opposite extreme, and enjoys the doubtful distinction of having been for some years after his departure the leader of an Antinomian party. Nor again was there much to be hoped from the goodwill of Mr. Giles Thorne B.A.,† who took occasion in 1629, when preaching a University sermon, to deliver a highly coloured philippic against Arminian doctrines. The moment was singularly ill chosen, for Laud had just been appointed Chancellor; and the offender had not even the grace to stick to his guns. The King, happening to be at Woodstock shortly afterwards, interfered in person; having summoned Thorne, with another culprit of the same kind, to appear before him, he decided that "the contumacy was notorious, and the sermon base." In spite of a most submissive petition addressed to Laud, Thorne was expelled from the University.‡ Having suffered a foretaste of the joys of martyrdom, he repented and reformed his behaviour to

* Crispe entered as a Fellow-Commoner.
† Giles Thorne was a Fellow of ten years' standing, and at this date one of the Bursars.
‡ He resigned his Fellowship in due form, November 29, 1630.

such good effect that he became a Bedfordshire incumbent, notorious for his loyalty. For this change of front he was rather roughly handled by Parliamentary soldiers, but at the Restoration obtained a *quid pro quo* in the Archdeaconry of Buckingham.

Allies so half-hearted were worth little to Puritanism in the hour of depression. Even these began to fail; for the Laudian party kept watch upon Oxford, and even in the smaller Colleges cultivated friendships with all possible diligence, both among the Commoners of good old families, and among those earnest thinkers on religious subjects, who found the Puritan formula inadequate for the solution of their difficulties. Both types were well represented at Balliol. The Commoners needed little inducement to stand fast in opposition to Parliament and the religious reformers. They belonged for the most part to those loyal county families which were afterwards to be the backbone of the Cavalier party; and even those whose future depended on their own abilities saw their best chance of rewards and honours in cleaving to the King. Of these pushing spirits Thomas Bushell is a fair example. Entering the College about the year 1608, he soon displayed so much aptitude for natural science that he won the favour of Lord Bacon, whose seal-bearer he became. On Bacon's fall Bushell had the happy thought to pay his court to Queen Henrietta. The gift of an ornamental garden with rock-hewn grottoes immediately won her favour; through her good offices Bushell rose to be the farmer of his Majesty's minerals in Wales. "He did cloath the King's army at Oxford with the produce of the said minerals," and afterwards having received a patent for the minting of silver money, " brought the said mint to serve his Majesty's occasions in Oxford, when his other mint in the Tower of London was denied him."

Scholars of the Arminian school began to make their appearance in Balliol immediately upon the election of Dr. Parkhurst. Among those who were eventually elected to Fellowships we find John Greaves, equally eminent as an astronomer, an Orientalist and a traveller; Lawrence, afterwards Margaret Professor and Master; George Linge, who obtained in 1638 the Bishopric of Cloyne, and in 1646 was nominated to the Archbishopric of Tuam, though the troubles of the time prevented him from ever enjoying the emoluments of the latter dignity; and Peter Wentworth, a cousin to Lord Strafford, by whom he was preferred to the deanery of Armagh. There were others too whose careers were less consistent, and who beginning as Arminians ended their lives as Romanists. Henry Savage, whose personal recollections covered this period, gives an amusing account of one such pervert, Elias Farely.

"Admitted to this College about 1617 where he proceeded B.A. But as soon as he had time for Master he crossed the seas and became priest in the Church of Rome, and at present he is said to be the chief favourite of the Popes, and in likelihood to be the next Cardinal. A while before his flight I heard him make an excellent oration before the Master and all the College, upon this theme, viz., *Achillis lacrimae Patroclum mortuum sic alloquuntur.* But at another time he declaimed upon this theme, *Propria quae maribus femineo generi tribuuntar,* for which he was justly reproved by the Reverend Master, Dr. Parkhurst, as arguing a levity of nature incident to those that change their religion."

A second was John Clabrook, "now at last advanced to the dignity of a Chanoine in some of the farther parts of France or Flanders"; but of him Henry Savage can only recollect that he was "a great Opinionatre," with the saving grace of honesty, "so conscionable that he took order for the discharge of the least of his debts here." His biographer is shrewdly of opinion that Clabrook would never have changed his religion if he had not been disappointed of a Fellowship.

Before we proceed to the story of the conflicts which arose out of this wild confusion of sects and opinions, a brief survey must be taken of the constitutional changes made in the years 1600–1640. The stream of pious bounty, which had been rudely checked at the Reformation, began to flow again as soon as a lasting settlement in Church and State appeared to have been reached. Early in the century the College was enriched by gifts from Peter Blundell, Mrs. Mary Dunch,* and Lady Elizabeth Periham. Peter Blundell was a wealthy merchant-clothier who had risen to opulence from very humble beginnings.

"He was at first a very poor lad of Tiverton, who for a little support went errands for the carriers that came to that town, and was tractable in looking after their horses and doing little services for them as they gave him orders. By degrees, in such means, he got a little money of which he was very provident and careful; and bought therewith

* Mrs. Dunch gave a single Exhibition charged upon her lands at North Merton. The charge was never paid after 1742.

a kersey which a carrier was kind enough to carry to London gratis and make him the advantage of the return. Having done so for some time he at length got kersies enough to lade a horse and went up to London with it himself. Where, being found very industrious and diligent, he was received into good employment by those who managed the kersey trade." *

Dying without wife or family in 1599, Peter Blundell left a large proportion of his savings in the hands of feoffees, to be spent in providing education for the boys of his native town. The sum of £2400 was appropriated for the building of a free grammar school to accommodate one hundred and fifty boys; £2000 more went to purchase lands for the maintenance of three scholars in Oxford and three in Cambridge. These scholars were to be chosen from Blundell's School, and natives of Tiverton were to have the preference over strangers. The object of founding the scholarships was partly to provide a career for Tiverton men, partly to promote the increase of "good and godly preachers of the Gospel."

Sir John Popham, an old country neighbour of the testator, was named among the feoffees, and it was specially directed in the will that the administration of the University scholarships should be left in his hands. He entered into negotiations with the Colleges of Emanuel and Sidney Sussex at Cambridge, and at Oxford with the Master and Fellows of Balliol. So far as Balliol was concerned the result was a Composition (1601), by which the Lord Chief Justice provided for the maintenance of a Blundell Fellow and a Blundell Scholar in that

* Prince, *Devon Worthies*.

House. The Fellow was to be a graduate, receiving a stipend of £15, which he lost on the expiration of ten years from his M.A. degree. The Scholar, who received £8, might keep his place until there was a vacancy in the Fellowship, and then would succeed to the Fellowship as of right. Both the Fellow and the Scholar were, as Blundell had desired, to read Divinity so long as they enjoyed their emoluments.

The Blundell Foundation, in this form, was altogether innocuous, and might possibly in the future be indirectly productive of advantage. Unfortunately Sir John Popham and his co-feoffees conceived it their duty to drive a hard bargain on behalf of the Tiverton men. In 1604 the Master and Fellows had to concede that the Blundell Fellow and Scholar should enjoy, in respect of rooms and commons, the same privileges as the members of the old foundation. Again in 1615 they were compelled to admit the Blundell Fellow as one of the governing body, and, worse still, to promise that if the Blundell Fellowship were not vacant at the time when the Blundell Scholar took his degree, then the latter should be entitled to the next Fellowship on the old Foundation. Respecting this arrangement a Visitor of the next century remarks with as much justice as severity:

"I am not less surprised than I was at first that there should be such a clause in the Tiverton composition, when the scholars on the old foundation have no claim to the fellowship on Blundell's. I cannot but think that the College was very condescending to grant such a clause."

Emanuel and Sidney Sussex were wiser in their generation, totally refusing to give the Somersetshire men such a claim upon them. The full effect of the mistake made at Balliol was only realised after the Restoration. In 1676 the feoffees agreed with the College that there should be henceforth two Fellows and two Scholars on the Blundell Foundation, and the West Country shortly afterwards acquired a majority among the Fellows which it long maintained to the infinite detriment of the College. No one would have grudged the preponderant influence of Somersetshire if it had been gained by open competition; but the Blundell men were rarely conspicuous in any way. They obtained their scholarships on easy terms, and were then certain to obtain a Fellowship, so long as their conduct was not absolutely flagrant. Even in a pecuniary sense the bargain was not, from the Balliol point of view, a great success. From Sir John Popham the Fellows received the sum of £700 to be invested in land, and in return they undertook to find the stipends of the Blundell Fellow and Scholar. But the Woodstock farm which they purchased with this sum disappointed their expectations. The highest rack-rent obtainable barely indemnified them for the new charges to which they were put. Sometimes they could find no tenant, and sometimes the rent could not be screwed out of the tenant. In 1676 about the same sum was received from the feoffees. The greater part of it was used to repair the College buildings, instead of being profitably invested. The revenues of future years were mortgaged in perpetuity to obtain a trifling advantage in the present. On the whole much more was lost than gained by the Blundell legacy, although indirectly it led to a close connection with many

Somersetshire families and although a number of small gifts were the result of that connection.

The gift made by Lord Bacon's sister, Lady Periham, was a less questionable benefit. Like Peter Blundell she was a stranger to the College, but her endowment was intended primarily for its benefit, and not for that of any particular school or locality. She asked her brothers, Nathaniel and Nicholas Bacon, to select for her some institution in the University which would be a worthy object of charity, and they, doubtless inspired by Archbishop Abbott, fixed upon Balliol. The Master and Fellows received from her two farms to provide for the maintenance of one Fellow and two Scholars. So long as she lived the benefactress reserved to herself the right of nominating the holders. After her death the Fellow and one of the Scholars were to be freely elected by the College; the second Scholar was to be nominated by the Periham Fellow for the time being. The Fellow was required to teach the two Scholars without fee or reward; his only other duty was to preach a memorial sermon in the Chapel on the first Sunday in May; but if he did not happen to be in orders the College might appoint some other preacher. Apart from these obligations the Periham Fellow stood on precisely the same footing as his colleagues. The first appointments on this Foundation were made in the year 1620. Henceforth the College comprised twelve Fellows (one Blundell, one Periham), and thirteen scholars (one Blundell, two Periham).

To construct lodgings for her pensioners Lady Periham allowed the sum of £50. If tradition may be believed the site chosen for these lodgings was on the north side of the back garden, facing the parish church, but all trace of them has long since disappeared. They are remarkable as being, after Hammond's lodgings, the first buildings which the College erected outside the front quadrangle. In 1623 a more notable extension was made on the same side of the garden. The site of the present back-gate was then occupied by a private house, the property of Sir Julius Cæsar, Master of the Rolls.* This was purchased for the sum of £300 at the moment when the Tisdale Fellows and Scholars, to the number of thirteen, were expected to take up their abode in Balliol.

Thomas Tisdale was a grazier and a native of Abingdon who, dying in 1610, left the sum of £5000 to found seven Fellowships and six Scholarships in an Oxford College for the benefit of Abingdon Grammar School. The Abingdon Corporation, to whom the final arrangements had been left, were at first persuaded by Archbishop Abbott to think of Balliol. Negotiations went so far that £300 changed hands, Cæsar's Lodgings were fitted up, and six Tisdale pensioners installed in them. But, in 1623, the Tisdale foundation was so much augmented by the liberality of Richard Wightwick that the Abingdonians thought themselves in a position to found a separate College. The result of their ambitious project was Pembroke College, to which James I. stood godfather. The blow to Balliol was a heavy one, for the Master and Fellows were called upon to refund the

---

* Caesar's Lodgings were demolished in 1851, when Jowett was Bursar, because of their ruinous condition. On the south side they were fronted by a block of buildings called Pompey. A view of these last hangs in the dining-room of the Master's House.

£300 which they had received. The treasury was quite empty, and the demand would have brought them to bankruptcy if Abbott had not paid the whole sum out of his own pocket. But there was the less ground for complaint, as the Abingdon Scholars had received a very indifferent welcome during their brief stay in Balliol. At the beginning of the Summer term, 1624, one of them, Crabtree by name, fell out with Moore, a Freshman of three weeks' standing, pulling his hair and calling him an undergraduate. This word of reproach was too much for the sensitive soul of Mr. Moore. He drew a knife and struck to such effect that shortly afterwards the victim died of his wound. Luckily for the homicide, benefit of clergy was still pleadable, and he was merely sentenced to be branded with the letter **M** upon the palm of his hand. Even this sentence was remitted by the Crown upon a petition from the Vice-Chancellor, the Mayor, and some other persons of importance.

The reader must not suppose that every Balliol undergraduate was of this noisy, brawling type. The reminiscences recorded by Evelyn in his diary breathe a gentle odour of respectability. The young Fellow-Commoner performs his exercises with moderate diligence, holds improving intercourse with one of the junior Fellows,* and laments that his tutor, Mr. George Bradshaw, is so much engaged in quarrelling with the Master, Dr. Lawrence, that he fails to bestow the proper degree of attention upon tutorial duties.† He

* This was Jas. Thicknes, or Thickens. El. Probationer-Fellow, 1639.

† In 1640 Bradshaw is punished for non-residence with the loss of his commons for two months.

submits with equanimity and mild approbation to the severe discipline imposed by Dr. Lawrence; he declaims before the Fellows in Chapel; in due season he goes with some others to be confirmed by the Bishop of Oxford in the University Church, " but this received, I fear, for the more part out of curiosity, than with that due preparation and advice which had been requisite." For recreation Evelyn went to the vaulting and dancing school; no doubt he also figured as a performer on the viol or the theorbo at some of those private concerts which were so fashionable in the Oxford of that day. During his first year his expenses were controlled by his tutor, but on reaching the age of eighteen he was allowed to manage his own allowance. Altogether, the three years which he spent in Balliol seem to have been one of the happiest interludes in a happy life. Evelyn formed there some lasting friendships, and he remarks with pleasure, when he returned fourteen years later, that " I supped in Balliol where they made me extraordinarily welcome."*

The College was at this time under the patronage of Laud, who, according to Savage, made it several gifts and received several letters of thanks in return. No trace of the gifts or the letters can now be found. But we may attribute the election of Dr. Lawrence as Master to the influence of Laud;† for Lawrence was regarded with favour at Court, became Chaplain to Charles I., and afterwards Margaret Professor of

---

* Evelyn gave to the College, besides the usual £10 for plate, several books for the Library: in 1697 he presented his own *Discourse on Medals*.

† Laud is first mentioned in the *Register* as sanctioning, in his capacity of Visitor, Dr. Lawrence's election.

Divinity. He was "accounted famous for scholastical divinity, a profound theologist, and exquisite in the excellencies of the Greek and Latin tongues." Under him the laxness of living, which Parkhurst had tolerated, was firmly suppressed. This and his pronounced Anglicanism are quite sufficient to account for the strained relations which existed between himself and certain of the Fellows. His chief opponent, Mr. George Bradshaw, is afterwards mentioned as the friend and spy of the Parliamentary Visitors.

CHAPTER VIII

THE CIVIL WAR AND COMMONWEALTH

Masters: Thomas Lawrence, 1637; Francis Cheynell, 1648; George Bradshaw, 1648; Henry Savage, 1650.

For Balliol the first result of the quarrel between Crown and Parliament was the loss of the most distinguished Visitor whom the College had ever obeyed. Laud, though he retained the Chancellorship until 1643, would appear to have broken off his connection with Balliol at least a year earlier; for in May 1642 it was resolved at a College meeting to send a deputation acknowledging Winstaffe, Bishop of Lincoln, as Visitor. A more keenly felt calamity was the total loss of the rents from the estates at Stamfordham and elsewhere in the northern counties. All these had been let on lease with a clause providing for the remission of rent "si Scoti omnia vastaverint." Now that there was actual war upon the Border the tenants claimed the full benefit of this clause, and not content with doing so raised claims against the College on account of the expense to which they had been put in finding quarters, supplies, and recruits for the English army.

But the full significance of the new troubles was only realised in Oxford when the King and his army arrived there in the autumn of 1642. Those exuberant loyalists who had already begun to toast the King with three times three, and to stock their wardrobes with buff suits of a military cut, had now the opportunity of learning by personal experience the character of the Government which they were determined to support. Until the year 1646 Oxford continued to be the headquarters of the Royal army, and the seat of that brilliant, witty, dissolute Court which gathered round Charles I. in his adversity. The honour was an expensive one. Charles ruled Oxford as he had wished to rule the whole kingdom, hardly deigning to recognise the rights of property so long as he was in a position to override them.

During these years the studies of the University were practically suspended. The lecture-rooms were converted into magazines for powder and stores. The faithful remnant of the Lords and Commons used the Divinity Schools for a Parliament House. Lectures, examinations, and disputations could only be carried on in the North Chapel of St. Mary's Church, and there were few who troubled to take part in them. The King held his abode in Christ Church. The best rooms in Merton were occupied by the Queen. Magdalen was given over to the King's gunners and the park of artillery. The trainbands drilled in the quadrangle of New College. The smaller Colleges found themselves saddled with the duty of entertaining a variety of distinguished persons of both sexes. The gardens of Balliol and Trinity, rather unluckily as it proved, formed no inconsiderable attraction to those whose applications for a lodging could not well be refused. Dr. Lawrence and his neighbour old Dr. Kettell of Trinity found the invasion very prejudicial to the established rules of discipline. Aubrey, who was then in residence at Trinity, says:

"Our grove was the Daphne for the ladies and their gallants to walk in, and many times my Lady Isabella Thynne (she lay at Balliol College) would make her entry with a lute or a theorbo played before her. I have heard her play on it in the grove myself; for which Mr. Edmund Waller hath in his poems for ever made her famous."

The respected President of Trinity, who had little music and less poetry in his composition, much resented these and other pranks of a more questionable character. One day, after Lady Isabella and her bosom friend Mrs. Fanshawe had scandalised the grave and amused the gay by attending morning chapel at Trinity "half-dressed like angels," he lectured them in good set terms, such as his age thought no shame to use. "Madam!" he said to Lady Isabella, by way of a peroration, "get you gone for a very woman." These heroic remedies were not to be expected from Dr. Lawrence, but the "honest, careful man," as Laud calls him, fretted inordinately over the derangement of his little realm; he fell into a settled state of melancholy, grew slovenly in his dress and negligent of all business. He made no attempt to save the College from ruin. It was used almost as a tavern by the Court and the soldiery. Every year, owing to their careless ways, the buildings grew more and more dilapidated. Money was beginning to be very scarce. In 1642 the College had to make an "extraordinary and voluntary loan" of the cash which they had in the treasury for his Majesty's use. Not the least extraordinary feature of the loan is that it passes without a mention in the Register, and, as the Bursar's Book for the year is missing, we do not know how much was lost in this way. Whatever the amount it could ill be spared. But this was merely the beginning of evils. In January 1643 the Master and Fellows surrendered all the plate with the exception of a chalice which they kept for the use of the Chapel. To the King the contribution can have been of small moment. When melted down the Balliol plate was valued at £41 4s., less than a seventh of the sum yielded by that of Magdalen. But, such as it was, the store represented the slow accumulations of a century; the loss, at a time when silver plate was one of the decencies of life, must have been severely felt. A little later in the year Dr. Lawrence, like other Heads of Colleges, was directed to inquire among the undergraduates whether any of them were willing to wear the King's uniform; they seem to have complied with the request as cheerfully as their contemporaries elsewhere. The Fellows, thus robbed at one stroke of the greater part of their remaining tutorial emoluments, were next invited to contribute according to their means to the maintenance of the army. Refusal was out of the question; they seem to have undertaken to maintain a single soldier apiece at the rate of four shillings a week. As if this were not enough an order was issued in 1643 that all the members of the University should present themselves with picks and shovels in the trenches, or should at least send substitutes if incapacitated for work of this kind. At this point some remonstrance was provoked; but the Colleges ultimately thought themselves fortunate to escape the new requisition on condition of paying a round sum of £40 per diem while the siege-works were in progress. In the end the army swallowed up nearly all of those who were not in orders. " Few there were," says Anthony Wood, "that went in Academical habits or formalities, for all under the age of sixty were upon military duty and therefore continually wore swords." The juniors addressed themselves to their new task with enthusiasm. Wood found them "to have been debauched by bearing arms and doing the duties belonging to soldiers, as watching, warding, and sitting in tippling-houses for whole nights together." They had the satisfaction of knowing that military service would rather help than hinder their academic advancement. In 1645 at the Balliol Fellowship election the choice of the College fell upon one Mr. Fielden, who was in the army of the King, and they decreed that he should be admitted whenever he found it convenient to return. Naturally the older men were less adaptable. Those who loved quiet or sympathised at heart with Parliament retired into the country to wait for better times, and did not return until the siege came to an end. What with the flight of the seniors and the enlisting of the juniors, Balliol was almost deserted by its proper inhabitants. The College had not even the melancholy pleasure of entertaining those former pupils who had been ejected from their livings and preferments for political or religious causes. Oxford was the last place in the world in which the disconsolate sufferer for his principles would seek a quiet asylum.

At length this state of things came to an end. In the spring of 1646 Charles fled from Oxford before the advance of Fairfax. The weak garrison to which he committed the hopeless task of defence were thankful to surrender as soon as they had satisfied the requirements of honour. Even the most loyal in the University must have heaved a sigh of relief when the Articles of Surrender were signed and the Parliamentary troops marched in. Too soon the Colleges discovered that they had merely exchanged King Log for King Stork. If the King had dipped into their purses, the Parliament was resolved to interfere with their consciences and constitutions. The Articles of Surrender contained an intimation that the University would be reformed; the threat was soon carried into execution. In 1644 a Board of twenty-four Visitors made their appearance, and among them were ten Presbyterian ministers, who, as their lay colleagues showed a wholesome reluctance to interfere with what they did not understand, speedily acquired the chief voice in the proceedings of the Board. The Visitation was inaugurated with a prayer-meeting three hours in length. Then the Heads of Colleges were invited to produce their Statutes, Registers, and Accounts, and any other documents which might be of service to the reformers. From among the Fellows of the several Colleges delegates were appointed to report upon the morals and political sentiments of their equals and inferiors. The spirit displayed by the Visitors is well illustrated in their choice of agents at Balliol. Among the three whom they nominated there we find Mr. George Bradshaw, the Master's inveterate enemy. Naturally enough, he and his colleagues succeeded in framing a lengthy list of malignants.

The Heads of Houses were not slow to resent this slight upon their authority. They adopted an attitude of passive resistance, simply declining to appear before the Visitors or to give them any information. The University as a whole rallied to their side. The Visitors had arrested the Vice-Chancellor, Dr. Fell; but his delegate, Dr. Potter of Trinity, summoned Convocation and proceeded with the business of the University as if the Visitors had been non-existent. The Professors, among them Dr. Lawrence, lectured with most unwonted regularity as soon as the Visitors sent them orders to desist.

Of course a struggle with the supreme legislature could not be continued with any hope of success. In November 1647 the Heads of Houses were called before a Select Committee of the Commons and reprimanded. The Visitors received power to depose the contumacious, and the greater part of the malcontents resigned themselves to the inevitable. In April the Rector of Lincoln set the example of compliance to the Visitors, and took the oaths required, namely, to have no correspondence with the King, his Council, or his officers, and to forbear the preaching of those doctrines which the Reformed Churches had generally condemned. The example was immediately followed by the Master of Balliol, though it must have grieved him sorely to abjure his favourite dogma of the Real Presence.

The difficulties of the Visitors were by no means at an end when the Heads were vanquished. The reputed malignants were not easily compelled to make an appearance; many of them, when at length they came, flatly refused to take the oaths required;[*] and it was

---

[*] Thus on July 14, 1648, a Fellow-Commoner of Balliol, being interrogated, answered: "I will not be so traitorous to my King as to acknowledge the pretended right and authority of his enemies."

easier to pronounce than to enforce a sentence of exclusion from the University. In fact, soldiers had to be called in to the assistance of the Visitors. The Balliol suspects, in particular, distinguished themselves by their resistance. On May 18 out of sixteen interrogated only three would conform. These were a Blundell Fellow, twenty years of age, a Commoner of one year's standing, and the College cook. Four Fellows and nine undergraduates made more or less unsatisfactory answers. In the course of the next six months three more Fellows were ejected, one of them being the Mr. James Thickens whose "learned and friendly conversation" had been the delight of John Evelyn. Loyalty was the only offence of Thickens; but against Mr. Spurway, his companion in misfortune, two charges, "non-submission and marriage," were alleged simultaneously, and we are left to guess which of them had the more weight with the Visitors. Three Scholars were expelled at the same time for non-appearance. The vacant places were filled by the Visitors at their own discretion. In 1648 they put in four Fellows and ten Scholars, in 1649 three Fellows, in 1650 three Fellows and one Scholar. There were then left only five Fellows who had been elected before the close of the siege. At length, however, the Visitors stayed their hand. It was well, for their nominees had not done much credit to the predominant party. In 1650 one of them, a Mr. Poore, who had been nominated to a Fellowship in 1648, was removed because "many articles of a foul and scandalous nature were alleged against him." Diffidence, however, had nothing to do with the forbearance of the Visitors. Their resolution was that, "considering the debts of Balliol College, they will forbear to put any Fellow of the old foundation into the said College until they be further informed concerning the debts thereof." In 1652 the elections were made, as of old, freely. The second and third Visitations, of 1653 and 1654 respectively, did little to disturb the peace of Balliol.

But by this time the Mastership had changed hands more than once. Dr. Lawrence liked the new order so little that he resigned in May 1648, and departed to a country living offered him by Valentine Walton, to whom, while a prisoner in Oxford, Lawrence had shown some kindness. To take the place of Lawrence the Visitors could find no one better than their colleague Francis Cheynell. In the words of an unfriendly critic, he was "non tantum fanaticus sed et furiosus;"* which, no doubt, specially qualified him to deal with a College of malignants. Cheynell, however, had ambitions. Before three months had elapsed from his nomination he accepted the more lucrative post of President at St. John's. He was followed at Balliol by George Bradshaw, whose elevation was announced exactly one week after Lawrence, his broken-spirited rival, had turned his back on Oxford for ever. Finally, in 1650, Henry Savage accepted the Mastership which he was to hold for twenty-two years. He was a man of some culture, a passable classic, a dilettante historian, with a taste for good music, good pictures, and good wine. That he presided over a nondescript body of Fellows with good humour and discretion must be admitted; also, it is an ungracious task to criticise the man who, besides

* Wood in his *Modius Salium* calls Cheynell "a buffoon."

restoring the archives, the Library, and the finances of the College to tolerable order, has left us in his debt for the first continuous history of the Balliol foundation. Still, one must express a wish that the convictions of Dr. Henry Savage had been a trifle less elastic. He was, indeed, one of those who, in 1648, had made difficulties about the merely "negative oath" not to assist the King, which the first Commission had demanded. But he soon reconciled his conscience to this test, and, moreover, put on enough of the Puritan to qualify for the degree of Doctor of Divinity. He commended himself to the Commissioners with such good effect that, in the writ nominating him to the Mastership, they go out of their way to compliment him on his piety and learning. Later on he did not scruple to become, with the Heads of some other needy Colleges, a suppliant for the bounty of the Protector. The sincerity of his conversion may best be gauged by a glance at the pamphlets with which he won preferment after the Restoration. In *The Dew of Hermon which fell upon the Hill of Zion* he argued, with great erudition, against the granting of toleration to Nonconformists. Not satisfied with signing in his own person the required declaration that he believed everything contained in the Prayer-book and the Thirty-nine Articles, he published "Reasons to show that there is no need of such Reformation of the public Doctrines, Worship, Rites and Ceremonies, Church Government and Discipline as has been pretended."

The Fellows of the Protectorate period formed an eccentric community. Amongst them all the most ludicrous figure must have been that of Mr. Nicholas

Crouch, who held his Fellowship from 1634 to 1690. He kept a diary, now in the Library, which covers the whole period of the Commonwealth and Protectorate. But there is only a single line allotted to each day; that line is more often than not a perfect blank; and the Fire of London is, perhaps, the only public event to which he makes any allusion. Still, the sparse entries which do occur are gems of self-revelation; they are worthy of a place beside Addison's *Diary of a Citizen*. On the Monday Mr. Crouch will write " Hodie me purgabam ;" on the Tuesday, " Male me habui." Then will follow a blank of several days; then "adii Abingdon cum domina Savage." It may be remarked that the Honourable Mrs. Savage (she was a sister of Lord Sands) is the first Master's wife who is recorded to have lived within the precincts of the College. It is gratifying to discover from this entry that, unlike some ladies in similar positions at Merton and elsewhere, she lived on terms of cordiality with the Fellows. Besides Crouch there was, for a short time, another oddity in residence, of the name of Edmund Ellis. He was the last of the rigid Puritans who entered the College during this period. He was put in as a Scholar in 1651, but he was freely chosen at the Fellowship election of 1655. Not improbably he acquired this dignity *jure haereditario*, for his father had been a Fellow a quarter of a century before this time. Of his intellectual calibre we form no high estimate from the tract which he published in 1660, being *Opinions of Mr. Perkins and others concerning the Sport of Cock-Fighting*. The result to which he comes is this:

" Though it be my opinion that the sport of cock-fighting

is absolutely sinful, yet I would not have thee think, as the Vulgar will be ready to say, that I esteem as unregenerate all those who are of a contrary opinion."

It may be more than a coincidence that Mr. Ellis resigned his Fellowship in the year of the Restoration. But if conscientious scruples drove him from the College, he soon overcame them sufficiently to accept a comfortable Devonshire living; nine years later we find him sending a handsome donation to the fund which was raised for paying off the College debts. With the possible exception of Mr. Ellis there were no men of strong convictions in the College at the time of the Restoration. If we may judge from their gifts to the Library, they were honest, harmless, indolent gentlemen, with a great taste for plays and romances. One of them, for instance, gave a commonplace book with long extracts from the veracious narrative of Sir John Maundeville. The most opinionated of them all was Mr. John Goode; but he was neither against the Church nor for it. According to Wood, "he was one of the three atheists that were accounted so twenty years before this." Perhaps he earned this reputation by his devotion to the philosophy of Hobbes, whose *Leviathan* he presented to the Library.

The Parliamentary Visitors had done their best to make Oxford an irksome place of abode for the worldly minded undergraduate. They tried to revive a number of wholesome rules which had long been more honoured in the breach than the observance; as, for example, that dinner and supper should be served and eaten only in Hall, and that the conversation at meal-times should be either in Latin or Greek. They forbade seniors and juniors alike to powder their hair, to wear vain knots of ribands, or to parade the streets in riding-boots and spurs. On Sunday every one below the degree of Master was bound, not merely to attend a sermon, but also to give some account of it and of his other religious exercises to the proper College authority. Tutors were ordered to hold frequent prayer-meetings for the benefit of their pupils. In some Colleges these rules may have been observed. But Henry Savage was not the man to give himself or other people much trouble if they were neglected. The general slackness which prevailed may be realised from a resolution at a College-meeting of 1657, that some steps should be taken to provide tuition for the Scholars by allotting each of them to some particular Fellow as his tutor. Apparently the Scholars had for some time past been left to gather up what crumbs of knowledge they could from the lectures of the Praelectors. A certain section of the Fellows regarded the Scholars merely as a useless drain upon the finances, and would have been glad to suppress them altogether. In 1655 it was proposed at a College-meeting (1) to reduce the number of Scholars to eight, (2) to suppress all exhibitions whatever as they fell vacant. Happily these resolutions were thrown out. Commoners who could afford to pay for tuition were, doubtless, better provided for; but there were few Commoners at this time. The only one of note is John Kyrle, the "Man of Ross," whose admission as a Fellow-Commoner is recorded in 1654. The casual visitor to the Old Library, seeing Kyrle's portrait there, might suppose that he had been a notable benefactor. Such, however, is not the case. The portrait in question was presented to the

CIVIL WAR AND COMMONWEALTH 143

Master and Fellows in quite recent times by a descendant of the Kyrles.* According to the various lists of benefactors which are to be found in the Library and the Bursary, Kyrle, during his residence in Balliol, gave merely a tankard of the ordinary size for Fellow-Commoners. Afterwards, in 1670, he exchanged this for the fine loving-cup which is still in use. The cup has a capacity of five pints, and weighed originally 61 ounces, but by repairs and additions the weight has now been increased to 67 ounces. It bears the inscription, "Poculum charitatis ex dono Johannis Kyrle de Ross in agro Herefordiensi et hujus Collegii commensalis." In 1685 Kyrle's name again appears as a benefactor to the Chapel; he gave towards the restoration of the floor and roof two guineas, "duos aureos de Guinea." From these facts it is evident that he remembered Balliol with some affection; still there were contemporaries who did much more to help her. His residence, indeed, was short. He entered in 1654, and he took his name off the books in May 1657. It is consoling to one's belief in human nature that he adopted the very unfashionable course of paying his battells in full before he left the College. His name figures nowhere in the lengthy list of debtors which was compiled by the Bursar in 1680.

The magnificent eulogy which Pope, in his *Moral Essays*, pronounced upon Kyrle's later career is too long for quotation. But the account given by the acrimonious Hearne may be less familiar to our readers. Hearne had many friends in Balliol, and was aroused by Pope's poem to make particular inquiries about Kyrle in Herefordshire.

* Mr. Rowland Prothero.

"Mr. Pope had the main of his information about Mr. Kyrle from Jacob Tonson the bookseller, who hath purchased an estate of about £1000 a year and lives in Herefordshire, a man that is a great snivelling poor-spirited Whig, and good for nothing that I know of. . . . To enable him (Kyrle) to perform these extraordinary benefactions he had a wood, which perhaps once in fifteen years might bring him in between £1000 and £1500."

One of Hearne's informants told him

"'twas all out of vanity and ostentation, being the vainest man living, and that he (Kyrle) always hated his poor relations and would never look upon them or do anything for them, though many of them were very poor."

But [Hearne cannot end without a back-blow] the informant was a

"crazed man and withal very stingy."

So much has been written about the violent changes in manners which followed upon the Restoration that it may be well to look at the other side of the shield. The eccentric Hannibal Baskerville of Sunningwell, who dearly loved to attend and to chronicle a gaudy, gives a picture of undergraduate Balliol in Protectorate times which is the very reverse of sombre.

"Now I may not omit remembrance of a custom they have in Balliol College when they keep an eminent *Act Supper*, which I saw being invited thither some years before the King's Restoration. And that was in the midst of the Hall, in the fireplace, they had planted an oak which they would hew a foot square or more with all his green boughs and leaves flourishing upright, but the bark of the body was taken off. This strange sight, it being hard to conceive how they got it into their room, with the music and the good cheer, made the entertainment very pleasant."

The Act, now chiefly remembered in connection with the Act term, was the greatest festival of the Academic year, corresponding to the modern Encaenia, though held somewhat later in the summer. On the first Friday after July 7 a general Commencement was held in all the faculties. The day following an Act Supper was given by the Inceptors in each faculty at the College of the senior amongst them. The Balliol Act Supper was remarkable for a custom which Baskerville omits to mention. This was the comic oration, of a more or less personal character, delivered by some junior in the character of the *Terræ Filius*. The custom in a chastened form still exists at All Souls, where the oration is delivered by the junior Fellow on All Souls Day; and there is a similar usage at Magdalen. It was almost universal in the seventeenth century; Wood mentions that he filled the part of *Terræ Filius* at Merton in his younger days. Balliol continued the custom until 1730; but the Act Supper and all its observances are now things of the past. The seventeenth century had a genius for creating convivial ceremonies; but in Balliol, at least, the last two or three generations have prided themselves on suppressing or ignoring these trivialities. The loving-cup, which is still handed round on the first night after an election to the Mastership, and on some few other occasions, is almost the only exception.*

* Even the Grace which used to be said when the High Table rose from dinner was abolished by Jowett (*Life*, ii. p. 21), because of its length and because a Scholar had to be kept waiting to take the

Clearly Balliol was ripe for the Restoration some years before it came. The only changes produced by it were that Mr. Ellis disappeared, and Mr. Thickens, the friend of John Evelyn, came back again, being restored to his place by a special writ from the Crown.

"Charles by the grace of God, king of England, Scotland, France and Ireland, Defender of the Faith &c. to the Master and Fellows of Bayliol College in the University of Oxford, and to every one of them greeting. Whereas James Thicknes Gent. to the place of one of the fellows of the said College according to the custom there used hath been ... duly elected ... and hath behaved and governed himself well quietly and honestly; Nevertheless the late Visitors of the College aforesaid, not being ignorant of the premises, the said James Thicknes without any just or reasonable cause from his place of fellow of the said College to the damage of the said J. Thicknes not small but great did remove; We do command you friendly enjoining you that immediately upon the receipt of this our Writ the aforesaid James Thicknes to his place of Fellow in the said College you do restore &c."

One other result, though confidently expected, the Restoration did not bring. The College asked for the repayment of the loan to King Charles the Martyr, and also for the price of their plate which had been melted down. Need we say that the College asked in vain?

responses alternately with the Master and Fellows. As it was probably written in the seventeenth century we give it in full at the end of the Chapter.

[NOTE.—THE COLLEGE GRACE.

Scholar. Benedictus est Deus in donis suis.
Resp. Et sanctus in omnibus operibus suis.
Schol. Adjutorium nostrum in nomine Domini est.
Resp. Qui fecit caelum ac terras.
Schol. Sit nomen Dei benedictum.
Resp. Ab hoc tempore usque ad saecula.
Schol. Tribuere digneris, Domine Deus, nobis omnibus bona facientibus ob Tuum Sanctum nomen vitam aeternam.
Resp. Amen.
Schol. In memoria aeterna erit justus.
Resp. Et ab auditione mala nunquam timebit.
Schol. Justorum animae in manibus Dei sunt.
Resp. Ne tangant eos instrumenta nequitiae.

Funde, quaesumus, Domine Deus, in mentes nostras gratiam Tuam ut tuis hisce donis datis a Johanne Balliolo et Dervorguilla uxore caeterisque omnibus Benefactoribus nostris rite in Tuam gloriam utentes in vitam una cum fidelibus omnibus resurgamus, per Jesum Christum Dominum nostrum. Amen.

Deus pro infinita clementia sua Ecclesiae unitatem et concordiam concedat, Reginam conservet, pacemque huic Regno Populoque Christiano largiatur. Amen.]

CHAPTER IX

THE RESTORATION AND THE REVOLUTION

Masters: Henry Savage, 1650; Thomas Goode, 1672; John Venn, 1678; Roger Mander, 1687.

NEVER were the coteries in Oxford society so sharply marked as in the half-century which followed upon the Restoration. The older men, it is true, were united by a certain feeling of comradeship more powerful than the recollection of all their previous differences. They had heard so many party cries, and had seen so little good come of them, that they desired nothing but to be at peace for their remaining years. In ten years the world had moved forward rapidly, and they were left in the rear of the times. The rising generation had new interests, new amusements, and even a new language. The most eminent Cavalier or Roundhead was to them simply "an honest old toast," whose ideas they did not understand, and whose company they found insufferably tedious. The ostracised naturally drew together, and did so with the more ease since few of them had been extreme partisans. For Oxford, after the passing of the Clarendon Code, was forbidden ground to the Independent or Presbyterian; and those who had suffered most for the cause of King or Church were for the most part dead or else too aged to think of resuming their University life. The younger men, on the other hand, were infinitely divided. There were the "smarts" who frequented the coffee-houses in the High Street, the scientists by whom the Royal Society was afterwards founded, the classics, more polished than profound, who gathered round Aldrich and Savile at Christ Church and at Merton; there were, again, the clubs of barbarians who swept the streets by night, disguised in flat caps and white aprons, tearing up railings and breaking windows, and their older counterparts who gravitated from the tavern to high-table, and from high-table back again to the tavern. As time went on political factions arose: Petitioners and Abhorrers, the Whigs of the Constitution Club, and the Tories of the High Borlace. The animosities which broke out between the different sets found vent in street-brawls and in the debates of Convocation. On all sides there was abundance of heat. But of the juniors as of the seniors it is true that high aspirations and ardent enthusiasm were completely foreign to their natures. The most serious pursued their occupations in a dilettante spirit. The old men rummaged in the Bodleian and the archives of their Colleges, while the young trifled with test-tubes and air-pumps, or argued over the Epistles of Phalaris. The spirit was the same in each case, though the results were rather different. An odour of stale claret pervades the books, the gossip, and the events of the time. Claret was the master-passion of those who could afford the luxury, and only went out of favour when the French wars made port the more attainable liquor.

The purses of the Balliol men did not permit of claret, and the Split Crow in Broad Street was more patronised by them than the expensive coffee-houses in the High. When Henry Savage was succeeded in the Mastership by old Dr. Thomas Goode, the sometime Puritan made a gallant but ineffectual attempt to suppress a practice so contrary to good manners and the Statutes of Bishop Fox. The account which Prideaux gives of his discomfiture is too good not to be quoted in full.

"There is over against Balliol College a dingy, horrid, scandalous ale-house, fit for none but draymen and tinkers. Here the Balliol men continually lie and by perpetual bubbing add art to their natural stupidity to make themselves perfect sots. The head being informed of this called them together and in a grave speech informed them of the mischiefs of that hellish liquor called ale, that it destroyed both body and soul, and advised them by no means to have anything more to do with it; but one of them, not willing to be preached so tamely out of his beloved liquor, made reply that the Vice-Chancellor's men drank ale at the Split Crow and why should they not too? The old man being non-plussed with this reply immediately packeth away to the Vice-Chancellor,* and informed him of the ill-example his fellows gave to the rest of the town. But Bathurst, not liking his proposal, being formerly an old lover of ale himself, answered him roughly that there was no hurt in ale, and so turned the old man going; who returning to his college called his fellows together, and told them that he had been with the Vice-Chancellor, and that he told him there was no hurt in ale; truly he thought there was, but now being informed of the contrary, since the Vice-

* Dr. Bathurst, the President of Trinity.

Chancellor gave his men leave to drink ale, he would give them leave too; so now they may be sots by authority."

When these were the diversions of the tutors, the pupils could hardly be numerous or distinguished. The Balliol Fellows never failed to exact from each Commoner whom anxious parents had committed to their care, the terminal fee of £1 which custom sanctioned. But with this payment the connection of pupil and tutor seems to have begun and ended. After 1670 some attempt was made to attract Fellow-Commoners to the College. The old rules of 1610 relating to this class of students were disinterred and somewhat softened in 1691, so that there should be no fear of over-rigid discipline to deter intending applicants. About the same time the Master and Fellows, anticipating a device familiar in our own days, paid their court to the great Headmaster, Dr. Busby, electing him as Visitor in succession to Bishop Barlow. But their ingenuity met with less reward than it deserved. A pamphlet on the state of the University gives twenty-five as the average number of undergraduates in residence at Balliol about this time. Baskerville comes to much the same conclusion. "Balliol College, as near as I can gather, may be with the Master about 34 or 40 persons, besides Cooks Butlers and such like." If in this estimate all the twelve Fellows are counted as in residence, it would give us no more than fifteen Commoners in the College. But, as a matter of fact, leave of absence was continually granted to any Fellow who could show a reasonable excuse. A Fellow who had resided in his probationary year was held to have fulfilled the strict requirements of the Statutes. Therefore Baskerville's calculation agrees fairly well with that given above and with the evidence of the Bursars' Books.*

Baskerville leaves out of account two classes of undergraduates who stood on a lower level than the Commoners and full Scholars. The Battellers received small allowances and performed some slight services in the House. In Chapel they sat apart from the other worshippers, and altogether were regarded as social inferiors; we may perhaps call them the minor Exhibitioners of the period. The amount which they paid in fees and Caution-money shows that they were not the matriculated servants of earlier times, and that their position was distinctly better than that of the servitors. Of servitors there was, according to the Register, an extravagant number; every Fellow had or might have several to attend upon him. Nothing can have been more wretched than their condition. The Scholars, indeed, had one menial service to perform, that of waiting upon the Master and Fellows at table. But the servitor waited upon the Scholars and the Commoners both in Hall and elsewhere. He made their beds, swept their chambers, carried water and coals, or did the marketing for the kitchen. In return he was allotted a garret under the roof, had the privilege of attending lectures, and possibly obtained a little tuition from the Fellow who was his patron. The pride of class was never so arrogantly asserted as at this time when social

---

* The Buttery Books would have given us more exact information; but they are in an extremely dilapidated condition and have never been arranged in chronological or other order; hence they are not available for purposes of reference.

distinctions were losing all political significance; the servitor was treated with all the more contempt because he usually belonged to a station in which menial service had become second nature. George Whitefield the Methodist may be quoted as a case in point. He was a drawer at the Bell Inn in Gloucester before he became a servitor at Pembroke, and the duties which he had to perform at Oxford were precisely those of his former avocation. The servitor, in short, was a social pariah with whom men of ordinary good sense and good feeling hardly cared to be seen walking and conversing in public. To what companionship he was driven by his isolation the following tragedy, enacted in Balliol, will show.

A certain servitor named White struck up a friendship with a plausible young reprobate, Thomas Howell, who had been a red-coat and was now the apprentice of a tailor in Broad Street, much patronised by Balliol men. Howell, after trading on the generosity of the servitor for some little time, formed an exaggerated idea of his resources, and hit upon a plan for robbing him. One day, just as the bell was ringing for supper in Hall, he came into Balliol with a hatchet under his coat, and went to the rooms of White, whom he found, as he had expected, on the point of going off to wait at table. Howell explained that he had come to get his friend to write a letter for him; whereupon White invited him to wait until supper was over, and so departed. In his absence Howell produced the hatchet and commenced to break open the trunk in which White kept his money. White, returning before his time, caught the thief in the act, boxed his ears, and heaped reproaches on him.

But the ex-soldier was desperate; the girl with whom he was in love had vowed that she would never marry him until he could provide a handsome wedding, and, for this reason, he was determined to have White's money at any cost. He therefore murdered his benefactor with the hatchet, beating his head almost to a jelly, rifled the trunk, and stole away. He was afterwards convicted, and sentenced to be hanged in the little enclosure, surrounded by railings, which stood before the College gate in Broad Street.*

The Scholars ranked in popular estimation but one degree above the servitor, and the name of Scholar was often applied indifferently to both. But the Scholars, strictly so called, came from a better class, being usually the sons of substantial tradespeople or poor country parsons. They spared no pains to emphasise their superiority over the servitor. The deference which they displayed to the fashionable Commoner, when they found themselves in his company, was only equalled by the arrogance with which they treated their poorer brethren. There is no need to describe the type further, for Thackeray has immortalised it in the person of Mr. Jack Tusher. Not unnaturally the Scholars were despised. Hannibal Baskerville names among his acquaintances in Balliol "Mr. Paine a scholler, the son of my loving friend Mr. Paine the apothecary of Abingdon." But that Baskerville, a man of means and of good family, should cultivate the society of such a person was only another proof of the eccentricity by which he was distinguished throughout his career.

* The story is briefly told in Wood's diary; but the account given here is taken from the MS. of Hannibal Baskerville.

RESTORATION AND REVOLUTION 155

In confirmation of what we have said on this subject the treatment of the minor Exhibitioners may be noticed. Those of Dr. Bell were treated as the servants of the Master; this was his reward for the pains of attending to their tuition. Some unspecified but distinctly menial services were also required of the Dunch Exhibitioners. There is in the Register a remonstrance on the subject which one of the Dunch trustees addressed to the Master and Fellows in 1663.

" Reverend Sir : I perceive by the demur of the party I have presented to you that, whereas he expected a scholarship he reputes himself entering upon a service, the very name of which, were the dewtyes lighter and less conspicuous, carries a blemish, especially with persons whose education hath been free and ingenuous. Sir, I must need confess myself concerned that the charity of my ancestors may be accepted as a courtesy by those to partake of it, and I know you are no less jealous of a reputation of faithfulness to the dead and their pious intentions, at least for the encouragement of the like example."

Shortly after the Restoration yet another coterie was added to those already existing in the College. Thanks to the bequests of Bishop Warner and John Snell, a number of Scotch Exhibitioners made their appearance. Both these benefactors were primarily concerned for the welfare of the Anglican Church in Scotland; they thought that they could do it no better service than that of securing a constant supply of educated clergymen. Balliol, the reputed foundation of a Scottish king, naturally commended itself to their notice as a likely training school. Unfortunately for the success of their plan, Balliol had long since ceased to regard itself as a Scottish College. The "blameless Hyperboreans" were not received with that cordiality which they had a right to expect. The Master and Fellows tolerated them as a source of income, but gave them the bare minimum to which they were legally entitled. The only occasions when the Snell and Warner Exhibitioners received any special assistance and protection from this quarter were, oddly enough, those on which they set themselves to defeat the purpose of their benefactors.

Bishop Warner of Rochester had during his lifetime proved himself a generous friend to Balliol. At his death in 1666 he not only left the sum of £50 to the Library, but also provided an annuity of £80 a year for the maintenance of Scholars of the Scottish nation who were to live and abide in Balliol College. The patronage of these Exhibitions was vested in the Archbishop of Canterbury and the Bishop of Rochester for the time being. They were tenable until the degree of M.A. had been taken; the one condition annexed was that the Exhibitioners should afterwards return to Scotland and there enter into Anglican orders. When the bequest was notified to Dr. Savage and his Fellows they showed no anxiety to claim it, probably because in the ruinous state of the buildings they doubted their ability to provide a sufficient number of rooms. The executors of the will decided that Gloucester Hall would be a more convenient residence for the Warner Exhibitioners. But Thomas Goode, on succeeding to the Mastership, persuaded himself and the Fellows that the Warner endowment offered advantages not to be despised. The executors of Bishop

RESTORATION AND REVOLUTION 157

Warner were induced to reconsider their decision, and the Exhibitioners were established in Balliol. The Colleges gave them rooms and other allowances on a more liberal scale than that observed in the case of ordinary Scholars. But soon complaints arose. In 1680 the Master and Fellows complained to the Patrons that the Scotchmen abused their privileges, ran into debt for their battells, and often left the College without discharging their obligations:

" and thoughe after their departure they made shift by importunity or Favour to procure the continuance of their pensions, yet they took no care out of those receipts to discharge the Scores which they had left behind them."

The condition of taking Anglican orders prevented the best men from coming forward. The Exhibitioners were compelled to give sureties, to the amount of £200, that they would return to Scotland and take orders; the Master and Fellows were forbidden to give them testimonials for any other purpose except that of procuring their ordination by a Scotch Bishop. Consequently the Warner Exhibitioners did little during the time of their residence to raise the intellectual standard of Balliol, nor, when they went down, did their subsequent careers add much to her reputation.*

The same conditions, backed by even more stringent penalties, were attached to the Snell Exhibitions. But the trust not being administered by ecclesiastical dignitaries, the terms of it were seldom or never

* After 1700 the Warner Exhibitions were very usually held concurrently with the Snell; but there were a good many exceptions. Hamilton, *e.g.*, failed in his application for a Warner Exhibition.

enforced in all their rigour. When about 1740 the Vice-Chancellor and the Heads of Houses raised a process in Chancery to compel the Snell Exhibitioners to conform to the doctrines and discipline of the Church of England, and to enter into holy orders, the Court refused to entertain the request on the ground that custom had sanctioned a departure from the intentions of the Founder.

John Snell was a Glasgow graduate of Ayrshire extraction who, migrating to England after the Restoration, had amassed a fortune while in the enjoyment of sinecures about the Law Courts. Sir Orlando Bridgman made him Crier to the Court of Exchequer; when Bridgman was Lord Keeper, Snell was his seal-bearer; and during Shaftesbury's Chancellorship he had charge of the Great Seal. Towards the end of his life he found a residence in Oxford, and the High Church atmosphere of the University seems to have inspired the scheme for which he provided in his will. After various legacies he left the whole of his residuary estate to maintain and educate, in any College or Hall of Oxford which the trustees might select, not more than twelve Scotchmen who had received some part of their early training at Glasgow. The Exhibitioners were to be selected by the Provost and Fellows of Glasgow University, and to hold their Exhibitions for ten or eleven years. The trustees selected Balliol as the most fitting College; the number of the Exhibitions was fixed at five, each worth £40 a year and tenable for eleven years. But the value of the Snell lands increased so materially that both the number and the value of these prizes were afterward augmented. In 1872 there were no less than ten, each worth £116 10s. per annum. There can be no doubt that the connection with Glasgow was and is of benefit to Balliol. It has brought into the College a number of men somewhat older than the ordinary undergraduate, and fitted by their experience of a Scotch University to act as a corrective to the monotonous uniformity of the type manufactured in English Public Schools. But for more than a century after their first admission the Snell Exhibitioners had to fight an uphill battle. Their frugality and the provincialisms of their speech exposed them to ridicule among the undergraduates; their industry did not very greatly commend them to the tutors. In 1744 the Scotchmen sent a statement of their grievances to the Glasgow Senatus, complaining that their treatment was uncivil and that they were habitually allotted the worst rooms in the College. The remonstrances of the Senatus merely elicited from the Master the reply that, since the Snell Exhibitioners had "a total dislike of the College," they might with advantage be removed somewhere else. In 1776 the hint was made more definite; the Master and Fellows suggested Hertford College to the Senatus. Fortunately the suggestion was never adopted. Had it been so the College which only a few years before had the honour of housing Adam Smith, would have been the poorer by the loss of Sir William Hamilton, and of Archbishop Tait, who for eight critical years was her leading Tutor. Even in Tait's days the prejudice against the Snell Exhibitioners was not wholly extinct. Dr. Jenkyns cautioned him during his first term to hold aloof as much as possible from "the young Scotchmen from Glasgow, who formed a set by themselves, not, in his fastidious opinion, of the most desirable or creditable description."

Whatever might be the indirect advantages of the Snell and Warner Exhibitions, they did nothing to relieve the pecuniary embarrassments of the College. Nothing can be more dismal than the picture of the College finances as drawn by Savage in *Balliofergus*. Most of the estates had gone to rack and ruin, not always through unavoidable misfortunes. The Fellows could not be blamed for the fact that their most valuable lands lay in the North and that the North had suffered more than most parts of England from the commotions of the Civil War. But in some other cases they had only themselves to thank. The Bursars were carelessly chosen and insufficiently checked; being free, under a by-law of the College, from all liability for losses except those incurred through exceptionally gross negligence, they had for some time past taken no pains to enforce the just rights of their Society. Some lands had been lost, they did not know how; some had been wrested from them without any serious resistance on their part. Savage, for example, though thoroughly familiar with the College deeds, is unable to find among them any record of the way in which Christ Church acquired the Synagogue and Jews' Houses bequeathed to Balliol by William Burnel. He can only note the fact that they are lost, and remark that if a price had been promised it was never paid. Again, in tracing the fortunes of Chimers Hall, given in 1310, he narrates how it was sold to Canterbury Hall in return for a rent-charge upon the manor of Newington; how, when the lands of the cathedrals were confiscated by the Long Parliament,

Newington, for some mysterious reason, was treated as a part of the Canterbury estates; and how the purchaser of Newington repudiated all liability for the rent-charge. The College agent, Auditor Squib, of London,

"told us that we were never likely to see it more, unless we bought some of the lands of the Church of Canterbury, and got it allowed upon the purchase. To this purpose a sollicitor was employed at Worcester House for the purchase of a Quit-Rent of about 30s. *per annum* upon a Manor in Kent, or some such other small matter. But since that time I never heard of the sollicitor or the business. It may be that the greediness of Purchasers went between him and Home; for then, having devoured the whole dishes of the Church, they were ready to fall together by the ears for the scraps."

It may be so, as Savage says, but the haphazard manner in which he and his colleagues went to work is even more remarkable than the disappearance of a solicitor with specie concealed about his person. The fact is that, although the College was in the habit of blaming for all misfortunes those who had administered the finances in the "late licentious times," the spirit of negligence had invaded the Society at a much earlier date, and was by no means corrected at the Restoration. For instance, the pleasant habit of omitting to pay one's battels, which had become usual during the Civil Wars, remained in vogue as late as 1665; the Bursars were seldom stirred to action until the deficit had reached considerable proportions.

After these facts we are not surprised to learn that, in 1662, when the Colleges were assessed for the poor-rate, Balliol could only pay half a guinea "to the work-

L

master and marshall of the beggars," as against ten guineas contributed by Christ Church, and that the highest estimate of the corporate revenues is £300, while the lowest is £100. Of the revenues about one-third went to defray the Master's stipend. But there was still worse to come. The Register in 1666 notes that houses belonging to the College, the annual rent of which amounted to £41, have been utterly consumed, "per horrendum illud et inflammatissimum Incendium quod majorem partem Civitatis devastavit Londini." One fellowship was immediately suppressed, but, in spite of that economy, debts rose by leaps and bounds, and creditors became urgent. In 1667 the College owed its butcher £50, and had other obligations in proportion to be met at once. There was no cash in the treasury; a third of the plate acquired since the Civil War was sent to be melted down; but it only realised the quite insufficient sum of £55. A subscription had to be raised among those who were interested in the College. Christ Church gave £295; Bishop Warner, Mr. Edmund Brough, and the Blundell Feoffees £50 apiece; a like amount was contributed by Dr. Busby, "Schoole-master of Westminster." In all rather more than £600 was raised, the most pressing debts were discharged, and the London houses rebuilt. But there were still many anxious moments. In 1681 the Master and Fellows gladly acceded to the suggestion of John Locke that they should let the best rooms in the College to the Opposition Peers, who were coming to the Oxford Parliament to support the Exclusion Bill. Shaftesbury had directed his friend to see if a whole College could not be had; and he obtained nearly all the accommodation he wanted at Balliol. Though the Master of this date, John Venn, was first cousin to one of the regicides, political sympathies in Balliol ran strongly against the Whig Petitioners, and for years to come " my Lord Shaftesbury " was the worst nickname which the undergraduates could bestow upon a reputed " Roundhead." But the opportunity of turning an honest penny by a political opponent could not be resisted. More than half the College was given up for the use of Shaftesbury's party. At the eleventh hour the Whig leader found for his own use a more convenient lodging in New College Lane ; but at his departure he joined with the Duke of Monmouth and some others in presenting to the Master and Fellows " a large bole with a cover to it, all double guilt, 167 oz. 10 dwts."

The Whig Peers cannot have found Balliol a comfortable residence. The buildings were in the most ruinous condition, and until the year 1700 no attempt was made to repair them. Thanks to private liberality, the interior of the Chapel was brought back to a tolerable condition between 1685 and 1689, about £200 being subscribed by various individuals for a new pavement, repairs to the wainscoting, and so forth. But the Hall, the Library, and the rest of the front quadrangle are tersely described in the Register as " falling to pieces through age." We can, therefore, well believe the story which is told of Dr. Bathurst, the contemporary President of Trinity, that in his extreme old age he was found sitting on his garden wall and throwing stones at those of the Balliol windows which had any glass left in them, " as if happy to contribute his share in completing the appearance of ruin." In 1700 the Visitor, Henry Compton, Bishop of London, came to the rescue; he gave out of his own purse the sum of £100 and induced Dr. Ratcliffe, the Court physician, to do the same. The City of Bristol also gave £100, but burdened their gift with a condition that it should be spent upon lodgings for the accommodation of their Scholars and Exhibitioners, of whom they had several in the University. This was the origin of the Bristol Buildings which stand at the corner of the back quadrangle, next to Fisher's Buildings and facing St. Mary's Church. They never served the purpose for which they were originally intended. A Bristol Exhibitioner appears on the books of the College for three years only, and no more is heard of him after 1704.

The Master by whom the work of reconstruction was at length commenced is Dr. Roger Mander, himself a notable benefactor to the College. Of his immediate predecessors, John Venn had neither energy nor influence, and Henry Savage, in whose days the want of money had been most keenly felt, was too much the victim of a comfortable apathy to go far afield in the search for assistance. After the great effort of 1667 he appears to have remained quiet and content. But Dr. Goode appears to have practised the gentle art of begging with much perseverance throughout his period of office. It was through his friendship with Dr. Busby that the latter was induced to become the Visitor, and to found the Catechetical Lectureship which remained in existence until comparatively recent times. Another proof of Goode's importunity is to be found embedded in Evelyn's correspondence. We find him reproaching Evelyn for not returning a satisfactory answer to a previous appeal; he intimates with some plainness that, owing to her losses in "the late wars and the dreadful fire in London," Balliol needs and expects to be liberally assisted by her former pupils. The reply of Evelyn is very modern; his expenses are so heavy that he does not know where to turn for ready money; his delay in replying was not due to negligence, but to the hope that, when his fortunes improved, he might make a really handsome donation; meanwhile he encloses a bill for £20 in proof of his good intentions. Goode's effort were not confined to friends of the College. In the Wood collection there is to be seen a curious circular which he addressed to the clergy and gentry of Worcestershire, inviting them to found fellowships for the natives of their county in Balliol, and alleging as an inducement the old connection of the College with Worcestershire, through which "it is commonly known by the name of Worcester College." But this and similar experiments produced no solid results. In 1676 he had recourse to a more desperate remedy. He arranged with the Blundell feoffees that if they would give £600 in addition to their previous present the College would undertake to maintain for ever another Fellow and Scholar from Blundell's School. To furnish the heavy rate of interest for which the College thus became liable, a Fellowship and a Scholarship upon the old foundation were permanently suppressed; the Blundell men entered upon the enjoyment of the allowances thus liberated. Though the Visitor consented to this transaction, it cannot be regarded as either honest or successful. An unwarrantable breach was made in the old foundation, and the capital obtained from the Blundell feoffees by no means sufficed to put the finances on a sound footing.

In spite of this blunder Thomas Goode deserves to be remembered with gratitude. It is no mere accident that from the moment of his election gitfs to meet the less urgent needs of the College began to pour in; when he had set the example of canvassing his successors were not slow to imitate him. In 1673 Sir Thomas Wendy, a sometime Fellow-Commoner, bequeathed to the Library a collection of more than eleven hundred volumes, valued at the sum (considerable for the times) of £600. Great additions were made to the College plate by other Fellow-Commoners, few of whom were content to contribute the statutory minimum of £5. Dr. Mander gave in 1692 the advowson of Bere Regis, and at his death in 1704, bequeathed, besides a considerable number of books, the sum of £370. The valetudinarian, Nicholas Crouch, followed the Master's example of munificence. John Blagdon gave a farm to support an Exhibitioner; Mr. Ducket gave the living of Calstone, Wilts. Richard Trymnall, Bishop of Bath and Wells, and a former Fellow, also gave a living in 1701. Henry Compton, in 1713, bequeathed no less than five. In this way the College became exceedingly well provided with ecclesiastical patronage—a circumstance which was of no little importance, since it prevented the Fellowships from falling into utter contempt. For some time after the Restoration the direct emoluments of a Fellow were little or nothing, but the opportunity of taking a College living recurred fairly often. This explains a fact which might otherwise perplex us, that in 1676 it was found necessary to forbid the practice of corrupt resignations, and that for nearly half a century the College was on its guard against this abuse. The unblushing frankness of the All Souls system was never known in Balliol; no Fellow might nominate his own successor. But he might be, and sometimes was, bought out by the parents of a Blundell Scholar who was awaiting the next vacancy. Such a case occurred in 1708; the Master and Fellows, who at the time had a sore feeling against the Blundell men, detected the fraud in time, and refused the offered resignation. How often detection was escaped it is impossible to tell. Resignations were certainly frequent at the end of the seventeenth and the beginning of the eighteenth century; and not infrequently they redounded to the advantage of Blundell Scholars. More than this we cannot say.

CHAPTER X

BALLIOL IN THE EIGHTEENTH CENTURY

Masters: John Baron, 1704; Joseph Hunt, 1721; Theophilus Leigh, 1726; John Davey, 1785; Bishop Parsons, 1798

Though so lately governed by the kinsman of a regicide Balliol was for the first half of the eighteenth century a stronghold of the most reactionary Toryism. No less than five of the Fellows had been expelled at the Revolution for refusing to recognise the change of dynasty, and those who had submitted were at heart of the same opinion as those who held firm. The non-jurors, though deprived of their fellowship, hung about the College and infected it with their own enthusiasm for the house of Stuart. In June 1715 Hearne mentions that he walked out of Oxford with three Balliol men to celebrate the birthday of King James III. Two months later he has a story to tell of an assault committed by some Balliol "scholars" upon a recruiting officer, who had the temerity to show himself outside their gate.* Their war-cry was "an Ormond, an Ormond, down with the Roundheads, down with the Roundheads." The

---

* Until 1772 there was outside the gate an enclosed space with trees, such as one may still see at St. John's. Here the Fellows used to sit in the afternoon waiting for the arrival of the mail-coach. In 1772 the enclosure was surrendered to the city to facilitate the improvement of Broad Street (Ingram, p. 11).

Fellows shared to the full in the prejudices of their juniors. In the year 1723 they elected as their Visitor Dr. Brydges, a Canon of Rochester, for no better reason than that he was the friend of Atterbury. The same reason induced them on the death of Dr. Brydges to elect into his place Sir John Dolben, a Canon of Durham, who is generally supposed to have financed the Tory Party with the proceeds of the famous "golden stall." It is true that on political questions, as on most other subjects, the Fellows of Balliol were frequently divided. Dr. Baron, who was Master from 1704 to 1721, appears to have been a stalwart Whig, and during his Vice-Chancellorship the Jacobites throughout the University were in a state of nervous apprehension. He had his followers and imitators; but the majority of the Fellows were, until 1760, more than half inclined to be Jacobites; and until the beginning of the present century the senior common-room was Tory in sympathies.

The College suffered much from its political character. At first, during the reigns of William and Anne, the Tory connection was highly advantageous. County families anxious to place their sons in a home of sound Tory principles naturally turned to Balliol. The number of Gentlemen-Commoners greatly increased. A benefaction-book in the College Library names more than seventy as having entered between the years 1701 and 1717; the special fees which they paid for their privileges formed a notable addition to the revenues. But with the accession of the House of Hanover this source of profit was dried up, as year by year the High Tory families became less numerous and less influential. The number of entries accordingly declined. In 1778 the Register remarks that the room-rents are rapidly falling in value, and that little remains when dilapidations have been repaired. Two years before this date it had been found advisable to suppress a Fellowship on account of the shrinkage of the dividends.*

It would be too much to say that the College was excessively poor. The Fellows individually must have been in easy circumstances if we may judge from the sums which they paid for their rooms and furniture. And in 1732 their commons had been increased with the consent of the Visitor, because a rise in the rents of the Northumberland property had left them with a surplus. But their policy, at least before 1789, was improvident. There was no reserve fund; all the profits of a good year went into the dividend. The necessity of making ordinary repairs was reluctantly admitted when walls cracked and ceilings began to fall. The idea that the general decay of the fabric must soon necessitate more extensive operations was obstinately put on one side. When, at the beginning of the century, the Master's House was built, the Master's stipend had to bear the greater part of the expense. Fisher's Buildings, the one other addition made to the buildings in this period, were, as their name denotes, erected at the charges of a private individual.

These buildings are still one of the most conspicuous features of the College, and though it is easy to cavil at the tasteless Italian style which the architect adopted, no Balliol man would wish to see them and their traditions swept away. It is in them that the College ghost has taken up his habitation. More than one

* This Fellowship was not revived until 1816.

From a Photograph by the] [Oxford Camera Club

FISHER'S BUILDINGS

belated reveller is reported to have met, in one of their rambling passages, the wraith of an old Fellow in eighteenth-century costume, wringing his hands and lamenting. The explanation of this grief is not given in the current stories. Are we to suppose that the excellent Mr. Fisher has in another world learned the first principles of architecture, and that he returns to mourn over his earlier errors of taste? Certainly he had no crime upon his conscience. He was a very worthy clergyman, who resigned his Fellowship to take the living of Bere Regis in Dorset. He had originally put the College down in his will for a handsome legacy; but his friend and neighbour Mr. Hutchins, the antiquarian (also a Balliol man), persuaded him that a gift to take effect immediately would be more acceptable. Accordingly Fisher paid down the sum of £3000 in the year 1767. On his death in 1773 he left the sum of £100 as a further token of goodwill; a tradition, which it would be rash to contradict in the hearing of a Balliol man, assures us that on his death-bed he requested the Master and Fellows to place on his buildings the motto "Verbum non amplius Fisher." The motto is there to this day, and is the subject of a well-known College song.*

With the exception of Fisher the College had, in the eighteenth century, no benefactor of any great note. In 1722 the Visitor, Bishop Robinson, bequeathed the Rectory of Mark's Tey, Essex. Two years later a Mr. Docton gave £800 to enable the College to purchase the living of Huntspill. In 1747 a former

* The same legend is engraved on Mr. Fisher's monument at Bere Regis (Ingram, *Memorials*).

Blundell Fellow, the Rev. John Newte, founded an Exhibition for natives of Tiverton. In 1779, a certain Mr. Wight, Vicar of Tetbury, made a bequest, on the following curious terms. On failure of the issue of his daughters the College was to take certain landed property, the revenues to be applied in founding a clerical Fellowship. The holder of the Fellowship was to preach annually four polemical sermons in Tetbury Church. In the first year he was to refute the Roman Catholics, in the second year the Presbyterians, in the third the Baptists, in the fourth the Quakers, in the fifth the Methodists, and in the sixth the Independents; after the sixth year the cycle began anew. The style of the sermons was to be "easy and familiar so as he may be understood, if possible, by the meanest capacity." The Master and Fellows acknowledged the bequest in suitable terms; but they probably reflected that controversialists of the kind desired by Mr. Wight would not be adaptable members of a common-room. The lands were never received, and consequently the Fellowship was never founded.

This paucity of bequests can hardly surprise us when we remark how little the College did for its undergraduates at this time. Except for one short period, 1713–1723, the tuition which it supplied was inefficient in the extreme. The number of lecturers was indeed raised from three to six; in 1697 two were appointed to lecture on mathematics and on the classical poets; afterwards a third was added for Hebrew. But their stipends were small and they treated their office as a sinecure. Adam Smith saw little or nothing of them or of his tutor when he was at Balliol (1740–1746). In the *Wealth of Nations* he remarks that no good teaching can be expected when the emoluments of a teacher are entirely unaffected by the degree of diligence or carelessness which he displays. The ordinary College lecture was merely a translation lesson. The audience construed, the lecturer listened; very occasionally the latter made a comment or reflection. Smith seems to have had little more than a bowing acquaintance with any of the Fellows; but perhaps his case was exceptional, for he was one of the unpopular Snell Exhibitioners, and never appears to have mingled much in undergraduate society. There never was a time when the College authorities were more ready to bow the knee before the social prejudices of their pupils. And Smith, moreover, had the misfortune to be caught in the act of reading Hume's *Treatise*; the fact, we may be sure, did not increase the goodwill of his tutor. But others who occupied a more normal position in the College, and that at a time when discipline and intellectual interests were reviving *pari passu*, tell us very much the same story as the great economist's. Sir William Hamilton (1807–1810) had for his tutor an eccentric being, Powell by name, who rarely emerged from his rooms in the tower above the gate, and never if he could help it took any notice of an undergraduate. Of the lectures Hamilton says in one of his home letters:

"I am so plagued by these foolish lectures of the College tutors that I have little time to do anything else. Aristotle to-day, ditto to-morrow, and I believe that if the ideas furnished by Aristotle to these numbskulls were taken away, it would be doubtful whether there remained a single notion."

Himself a Scotch Exhibitioner, Hamilton was, however, more fortunate than Smith, in that his superiors, if they did not help him, were at least encouraging, and took a visible pride in their remarkable pupil. Live and let live was their maxim. Southey's tutors, though they made him write Latin verses on King Charles the Martyr, treated his schemes of Pantisocracy with whimsical tolerance. "Mr. Southey," said one of them, "you won't learn anything from my lectures, Sir, so if you have any studies of your own you had better pursue them." The policy of *laissez faire* had some advantages for the pupil as well as for the tutor. There was at least no fear that original minds would be ground down to the pattern of mediocrity. But forty years before the time of Southey and Hamilton, when tutorial indolence was not incompatible with a jealous suspicion of new ideas, there can have been little good to say of the collegiate system.

It is true that the whole University was a prey to apathy during this period. But Balliol appears to have been rather below the average. Lord Melbourne said that what he liked in the Order of the Garter was that "there was no damned merit about it." In this respect at least, a Balliol Fellowship about the year 1750 ought to have been regarded as the blue ribbon of the University. The examinations were open to Bachelors from other Colleges, but, on one ground or another, the College usually decided in favour of its own candidate. It was at one time a widely held opinion that any scholar who acquitted himself tolerably in the examination ought to be preferred to the most brilliant stranger. Some ingenious spirits went so far as to suggest that when Fox made *extranei* eligible, he used the word in a special sense, to denote the Commoners of Balliol as distinguished from the Scholars; and although this theory, as a theory, was promptly scotched by the Visitor to whom it was referred, it continued for some time to influence the votes at elections. If the scholarships and exhibitions had been awarded on an open examination, the evil would have been less serious. But the foundation scholarships were in the gift of individual Fellows, the Dunch Exhibitioner was appointed by the heirs of Sir William Dunch, the Newte Exhibitioner by the three rectors of Tiverton, and so on through the list. There was, therefore, no guarantee that the Scholar or Exhibitioner would have the slightest tincture of ability. Often he had not. Still the older generation among the Fellows would vote for him. When reprimanded by the Visitor for partiality they fell back on the excuse that they could not find it in their consciences to vote for young men from other Colleges, who were indeed very clever scholars, but whose moral character might, for aught they knew, be most indifferent. When these principles were avowed by the examiners, the examinees not unnaturally treated the papers which they had to write as a farce. When, in 1780, an unsuccessful candidate, who had appealed to the Visitor, was charged with obtaining assistance in his Demosthenes, he retorted that "a Proposal was made to me by the other candidates of a *Mild Examination*, as they called it, and of carrying up a Lexicon," but that he had virtuously declined to be a party to any such fraud. In 1787 the Master himself took up the cudgels against the advocates of free competition. "On a review of the Elections that have been made for many years past, I cannot but express my astonishment at them." His astonishment is due to the fact that some of the Fellows have fallen into the habit of voting for outsiders.

"It cannot but be attended with a very untoward influence on the welfare of the College that it may be, and I am told has been said in the country that there is no encouragement for a parent to send his son to Balliol, as the preferments within the House are constantly bestowed on foreigners."

This was written at the time when the elections were beginning to be more conscientiously conducted, and immediately after four or five of those who assisted to reform the College had found their way into the Common-room. But how little ground the Master had for his fears may be judged from the choice which the Fellows made in 1783. Four Bachelors of Arts from other Colleges had presented themselves; one was Parsons, the future Master, who was the most distinguished man of his year; the other three were all men of known ability. The electors, however, rejected all of them and took a scholar of two years' standing, who was under twenty years of age, and of very inferior attainments. The Visitor, very much to his credit, quashed the election on an appeal, but the Fellows were quite prepared to repeat the offence at the earliest opportunity.

Among the Fellows the Tiverton men were the worst

offenders in the matter of elections. In 1732 there were fourteen Fellows in all: seven of them were from Blundell's School, and the Visitor intimated, with some plainness of language, his conviction that they habitually voted for their compatriots, without regard to the more important questions of good conduct and scholarship. Balliol, he said, was fast degenerating into a county college. The Master could only make a very lame reply to the impeachment. It is a melancholy consolation to think that the College was not altogether to blame for this tendency. The Blundell composition gave the trustees the power, which they never failed to use, of insisting that Tiverton scholars should be elected to the first vacancy on the old foundation when no Blundell fellowship happened to be available.* Complaints from the College on this head are frequent. In 1706 the Register records that "Henry Fisher, B.A., was nominated to a Fellowship, notwithstanding the statute *De eligibilis et probandi circumstantiis*, because the Blundell feoffees vehemently insisted." Not content with this remark the secretary adds, "Lest this should hereafter be to the greatest injury of the College, *nate cave dum resque sinit tua corrige vota*." A few years later the Fellows had a hard battle to exclude one William Cruwys, who was even more notoriously unfit than Fisher. William Cruwys had been expelled the College because, in the words of the Register, *fuit sicut fucus aliena devorans, nihil aut parum profecit, et spretis omnium meliora studentium monitis vitam diu egit improbam et a scholastica disciplina abhorrentem.* Seven years later, in 1718, he made his

* *Supra*, p. 123.

appearance to claim a vacant Fellowship. After a long argument the Visitor, Bishop Robinson, was persuaded to uphold the refusal of the College. But the danger to be faced on this occasion was a double one. Contrary to all precedent the Visitor invited the Vice-Chancellor and Heads of Houses to assist him in hearing the appeal of William Cruwys.* It was with the greatest difficulty that the establishment of a precedent so dangerous to the liberties of the College was avoided. When appeals might be attended with unexpected troubles of this kind, it is not surprising that the Master and Fellows seldom had the courage to fight the Blundell Scholars, and rather preferred to accept an unwelcome colleague than to imperil their whole constitution. The rooted aversion with which Balliol has, of late years, regarded local exhibitions is amply explained by the secret history of the Senior Common-room in the eighteenth century.

It must be admitted that the College was not fortunate in its masters. Little is known of Dr. Baron, but that little does not give a favourable impression of his character. He was on bad terms with the Fellows, and Dr. Stinton, among some Balliol reminiscences, informs us that

"Dr. Baron, being a factious man, would allow only one Copy of the Statutes in the College which he kept himself. Mr. Sanford being then a Fellow contrived to borrow Baron's copy, and shutting himself up in his room began to transcribe it. Dr. Baron, thinking he kept it too long, and suspecting what he was doing, sent for the Book. But Mr. Sanford, answering that he had not yet

* Rawlinson, MSS. B. 376, foll. 49, 156–9 (Bodleian).

done with it, and that the Master should have it the next day, went on with the transcript, and did not go out of his room till he had finished the whole."

Dr. Hunt, the next Master, was a confirmed invalid, most of whose time was spent at Bath and other health resorts. The College was tolerably well governed in his time by the Vicegerent whom he nominated, a senior Fellow of the name of Best. Best was an excellent man of business and enjoyed the reputation of a successful tutor. It was generally expected in the University that he would be Hunt's successor, and there was no more suitable candidate in the field. Unfortunately, his rather masterful government had gained him the ill-will of half the Fellows, and to keep him out they procured the election of Dr. Leigh, a young Corpus man, whose chief merit was his relationship to the Visitor. The immediate result was that the defeated Best left the College; with his departure the tutorial system collapsed, and, during the fifty-nine years for which Dr. Leigh ruled the College, educational duties were systematically neglected.

The details of this election throw a lurid light upon College politics in the eighteenth century. It attracted considerable attention in the University, and is casually noticed by Thomas Hearne in his diary. But Hearne gives only one side of the case. Dr. Leigh was one of the few Oxford men with whose politics he could unreservedly sympathise, and the election, as a triumph for the High Tory party, commanded his unqualified approval. The true history of the business we owe to Dr. Leigh himself, who with a superb indifference to the opinion of posterity, collected, and placed in the archives, all the correspondence bearing upon the election.

Immediately on the death of the old Master, the friends of Mr. Best began to canvass for supporters. The other party were surprised to receive visits from the parents of undergraduates, who intimated very plainly that their sons would be transferred elsewhere if Mr. Best were not elected. It seemed as if there were only one candidate who could take the field against Best with any chance of success, and this was the highly popular Visitor. To him, therefore, Best's opponents addressed themselves.

"The death of Dr. Hunt," they wrote, "is much lamented by all that knew him, but his loss will be the less felt by our Oxford friends, if the Visitor will so far degrade himself as to accept of the Mastership."

The Visitor appears to have been tempted by the suggestion. But he was cruelly disillusionised when he received from the other side a formal notice that his election would be opposed as illegal.

"As we can't be so vain as to imagine the Headship of Balliol any ways worthy the acceptance of the Hon. Dr. Brydges, so do we apprehend that the Master's place of our College is inconsistent with that relation which, in your great kindness and condescension, you have already submitted to honour us with."

Dr. Brydges—a good, quiet man, devoted to his manuscripts and medals—hastily resigned the idea of confronting this opposition. But his *amour propre* had been wounded, and he gladly accepted the suggestion that his nephew, Theophilus Leigh, should contest the election.

When Dr. Leigh and his friends reviewed the situation, they found that the votes would in all probability be equally divided. Six of the Fellows were for Mr. Best, and six for his opponent. On each side there was one doubtful vote. Mr. Lux, the senior Fellow, who was for Best, was commonly reported to be out of his mind, but the truth could not be ascertained, because his rooms were garrisoned night and day, and no inquisitive eyes were allowed to inspect him. Mr. Quick, one of the juniors, and a friend of Dr. Leigh, might be challenged because he had omitted, on his election, to subscribe the Act of Uniformity; it was possible that he might on that account be held *pro non-socio*.

The last few days before the election were spent by the one party in fruitless attempts to enter the rooms of Mr. Lux, and get him certified a lunatic; by the other in threatening Mr. Quick with deprivation as a non-juror. When the Fellows actually met in Chapel, an indescribable scene ensued. By the Statutes they were required to withdraw to the ante-Chapel, and to re-enter one by one for the purpose of delivering their votes to the Scrutators. But Mr. Lux, in virtue of his seniority, had to act as one of the Scrutators, and, although he was perfectly sane, the brutal tactics of his opponents had thrown him into such a state of excitement that his friends could not trust him out of their sight. His fellow Scrutators, if left alone with him, would probably have entrapped him into words or acts sufficient to constitute a legal proof of imbecility.

Accordingly, the party of Mr. Best announced that, while they were prepared to retire out of earshot, they would not quit the Chapel. After an ineffectual protest from the other side the election proceeded, and the votes were found to be equally divided. But Mr. Best and his friends claimed the victory on the ground that Mr. Quick's vote, being that of a non-juror, could not be counted, and that, even if it were admitted, he, as the junior Fellow present, was bound by the Statutes to cross over from Leigh's party and join theirs in order to make a majority. Without further formalities they left the Chapel, and carried off their candidate to take possession of the Master's Lodgings. But the minority, remaining behind, resolved unanimously that the election was void, proceeded to vote anew, and elected Dr. Leigh. Thus there were two Masters elected on the same day, and the Visitor was left to choose between them. Of the influences which were brought to bear upon his judgment there is an amusing specimen in the archives. A certain Mr. R. P. writes to the Visitor to the effect that Dr. Leigh is a Whig in disguise, that he was put up by the Duke of Chandos, acting in the interest of the Government, and that an honest Tory like Dr. Brydges ought to defend the Tory party against these unprincipled attacks. "Let Whig visitors go on to oppress and to judge wrong, but let all honest men do justice to their king and fellow-subjects." The argument was quite of a kind to command the attention of the Visitor, but, unfortunately for the success of his correspondent's special pleading, he knew his nephew Leigh to be a Tory of the soundest kind, whom no Whig Government was in the least likely to favour. His political duty coincided with his private inclination. Dr. Leigh was declared duly elected; he came into Oxford on March 21, 1727, accompanied by an immense troop of sympathisers, and made a public entry into the Master's house, which Mr. Best had only just evacuated. The defeated candidate swallowed his humiliation and kept his Fellowship until the next College living fell vacant. Though he had shown to little advantage in the contest, the College suffered by his loss. He was the one efficient tutor which it possessed, and no one could be found to fill his place.

A Master elected as Dr. Leigh had been could hardly expect to find the College unanimous in his favour. For the next sixty years the Senior Common-room simmered with discontent. Almost every election to a Fellowship provoked an appeal, and the contending factions did not spare one another in their pleadings. There is in the Register a severe letter from Dr. Brydges' successor, in which the Fellows are reprimanded for their evident animus against the Master. "As you seem to be jealous of your *Liberties*, so on the other hand it is not fitting that the Master, whom you acknowledge to be a principal and vital part of your Society, should be a Cypher in his own College."

The best excuse for the Fellows was the character of Dr. Leigh himself. Habitually and as a matter of course he sided with the more wrong-headed reactionaries. He defended the system of close fellowships, he excited in the College a prejudice against the harmless and industrious Scotchmen of the Snell foundation, and did his best to perpetuate among the younger generation the principles of Bolingbroke and Atterbury. It was inevitable that the advocates of any reform should be at war with him. Unfortunately the tradition of quarrelsomeness survived him. For a generation after his death the two factions in the Common-room were hardly on speaking terms. In 1806 a very worthy Bursar, a close friend of Dr. Parsons, is portrayed in an appeal to the Visitor as

"a Person who has resided for but a short time within the walls of our society, and during that residence has done little as a Tutor and nothing as a lecturer: who has indeed reappeared among us for the purpose of superintending the general accounts, but even in this subordinate service has seldom acted in private without a prompter, and never appeared in public life but as an Amanuensis."

His replies to their questions displayed an utter ignorance of his business, and "were expressed in a tone that sufficiently justified his claim to mental Imbecility."

Among the Commoners of the College Dr. Leigh's example led to more amusing ebullitions. He is particularly mentioned as the first clergyman who ever joined the Tory wine club which, under the cabalistic name of the High Borlace, met annually on August 18 at the King's Head Tavern, to drink the health of the Pretender, and confusion to the Whigs of the rival Constitution Club. No member of a Whig College, however unimpeachable his private sentiments, might be admitted to these innocently treasonable festivities, and Dr. Leigh was especially careful that his College should not disgrace him in the eyes of the Club. As the greater number of his Commoners hailed from the loyal cider-counties, they were not slow to take the tone which he desired. In 1745 the fashionable clique of the College were as exuberantly Tory as their fathers had been in 1715. Even the disaster of Culloden failed to quench their ardour. For some years after the final extinction of their hopes they continued to atone for the noisiness of their wine-parties by the soundness of the sentiments with which they accompanied their toasts; until at length a piece of more than ordinary indiscretion on their part attracted the attention of an irritable Government, and resulted in the prosecution of the chief offenders. They had been entertaining some boon companions in the College, on the occasion of the Cardinal York's birthday; and the evening being a warm one nothing would content them, after they had imbibed a sufficiency of port, but to stroll arm in arm down the High Street, shouting with all the force of their lungs, "God bless King James! Prince Charles! D—mn King George!" The tumult disturbed a Canon of Windsor who was sitting in Winter's Coffee House, and he, being an officious person and a Master of Arts, took upon himself to reprove them. But, as several of the gentlemen to whom he addressed himself "pulled off their cloaths" with evident bellicose intention, the self-constituted censor threw dignity to the winds, and ran for shelter to Oriel College. There he remained for some time, while his pursuers, to the number of thirty or forty, howled insults at him from the street outside. When at length Mr. Blacow summoned up the courage to emerge and make a dash for his lodgings, he found the way blocked, and there was another exciting scene. A truculent gentleman stepped forward in his shirt-sleeves and threw down the glove. "I am a man who dare say, God bless King James the Third! and I tell you my name is Dawes of St. Mary Hall. I am a man of independent fortune and therefore care for no man." At this juncture the Proctors came to Blacow's rescue, and the crowd dispersed. This however was far from ending the episode. Mr. Blacow, who had confidently expected the condign punishment of the offenders, discovered to his disgust that Dr. Leigh had talked over the Vice-Chancellor and the Proctors. The ringleaders escaped with a slight imposition, the others went scot-free. On receiving a formal complaint from Mr. Blacow, the Vice-Chancellor replied that young men would be young men, particularly when they were in liquor. The Attorney-General proved more sympathetic. On the information of Blacow Mr. Luxmore and Mr. Whitmore of Balliol, together with the courageous Mr. Dawes, were indicted in the Court of King's Bench. After a trial which lasted eight hours Mr. Luxmore was acquitted; but the other two were condemned to be imprisoned for two years, to find security for their good behaviour for seven years, and to go round immediately to all the Courts in Westminster Hall, with a paper on their foreheads detailing the particulars of their offence. Which sentence, says the reporter, was strictly executed.

The interior of the College, as may be imagined from the foregoing narrative, was the scene of some stirring episodes. On one occasion we find that a Commoner is rusticated because he challenged certain scholars to fight, and put them " to extreme peril of their lives." In 1779 the Register gives a lengthy account of a riot raised by Mr. Merry, a Scholar, and Mr. Parkinson, a

Commoner. About seven in the evening these two gentlemen appeared in the quadrangle in a state of uproarious intoxication. When ordered to their rooms by the Dean they jeered at him, and made a rush for the gate. The Dean called to the porter to lock it, which he did with great promptitude, but was assaulted for his pains. Then the offenders turned on the Dean, and cursed him forcibly and fluently. For this they were rusticated, but first compelled to make a public apology in the Chapel after morning service. It is not without significance that the sobriquet " men of Belial" first won its way into general use about this time.*

The favourite amusements of the College at this time were hunting, riding, and shooting. This probably explains the strict decree of 1757, which forbids the bringing of dogs, on any pretext whatever, within the College walls. For those who followed such pastimes reading of any kind must have been difficult; the hour of the hall-dinner was three o'clock, and, before that important event, it was necessary not only to don the full dress of swallow-tail coat, knee-breeches, silk stockings and pumps, but also to have one's hair powdered by the College barber, who began his operations on the junior Freshman a couple of hours before dinner, and worked steadily up the list to the Senior Fellow. Southey was the first who ventured to break the custom. He came into Hall with his long hair curling naturally over his shoulders, an innovation which rapidly commended itself to his contemporaries.

* *Terrae Filius* 1733 (Amherst). " The worthy Head and Men of *Balliol* (I mean *Belial*, for I believe it should be so spelt, since they are wicked enough to deserve that Title)."

The reading men kept to their rooms during the entire forenoon, and took their recreation afterwards by sailing on the river or walking in the country. Early in the century there was a fives-court in the back-quadrangle; but even the site of it was forgotten by the year 1800. Sir William Hamilton brought pole-jumping into fashion. He and his friends would start across country from Port Meadow or Bagley Wood, taking every obstacle which came in their way. Of Hamilton the story is told that one day, when walking past the Fellows' garden, he remembered that mulberries were in season, and took a flying leap over the high wall which then surrounded the mulberry-tree and the garden. To his consternation he alighted almost on the toes of the gouty Dr. Parsons, who happened to be taking his constitutional on the gravel walk. But the Master was so much impressed by the agility of his favourite pupil that he condoned the offence. Southey's less robust circle of friends were distinguished by their love of music. One had a fiddle, the strings of which were generally dilapidated, another had a flute, and a third imported a harpsichord into his room. But they seem to have been exceptional beings in every way. One of them turned teetotaler and refused to eat butter, because wine and butter were unknown in the state of Nature. Southey, who thought all the world but himself incorrigibly idle, rose at impossible hours in the morning to read, and characteristically enough spent a good part of the time thus gained in making hot negus to sustain the inner man. In his day late hours were already coming in: we hear nothing from him of the "laudable practice" which Pointer had noticed at the beginning of the century, that the Dean should visit every room at nine o'clock to see that all was quiet for the night. There was still, however, a closer degree of surveillance than would be considered necessary to-day. On this subject there is a story, long current in the College, and generally told of Sir William Hamilton. A late party in his rooms was disturbed by a noise at the door. Hamilton rose, flung the door open, and disclosed the figure of his tutor kneeling outside, with his ear where the keyhole had been a moment before. In a twinkling the spy was clutched by the collar and suspended over the well of the staircase, until his reiterated cries for mercy made it impossible to keep up the feint of non-recognition. He was then gently restored to *terra firma* amid a chorus of apologies: " We never dreamed for a moment that it could be you, Sir!" The tutor in question is said on the best authority to have been no other than Dr. Jenkins. If this is really the case, it speaks volumes for Jenkins' real goodness of heart that he completely lived down so unfortunate an incident.

From the commencement of the eighteenth century the Common-room played an important part in the social life of the College; for, although primarily intended as a meeting-place for the Fellows, it was open to Fellow-Commoners, and perhaps some of the more privileged among the other undergraduates; there is a decree in the Register forbidding these junior members to take their breakfast in the Common-room. A junior Common-room did not exist until the end of the century, and when founded soon came to an untimely end. Dr. Parsons, who regarded it as a centre of drunkenness and disorder, sent for the president and asked if it was true that such a society had been formed. Answered in the affirmative he asked to see the book of rules; and when they were produced solemnly put them on his study fire. Before this experiment there seems to have been a practice of using the Hall as a clubroom at night. Southey says:

"The old Hall had its central fire, and every member of the University had a right once a year to spend an evening there, and to be treated with bread and cheese and beer, and all on condition that when called upon he should either sing a song or tell a story."*

By the "old Hall" he means the modern Undergraduates' Library as it was before Wyatt undertook the restoration of it.

The jealousy with which the authorities regarded the attempt to found a junior Common-room had a curious reason underlying it. In Balliol, as doubtless in other Colleges, there was a nervous anxiety lest the undergraduate should get out of hand; and any attempt at combination for the most innocent purposes was regarded by the tutors as an underhand device for obtaining self-government. They feared a club as a mediæval statesman feared a commune, as Lord Eldon feared a trades union. Thus in 1699 a College meeting, after forbidding extravagance in the matter of degree suppers, which was a reasonable and necessary measure, went on to prohibit altogether the practice of sconcing on the ground that undergraduates should not be allowed to legislate for themselves. This is hardly the place to

* *Commonplace Book*, iv. p. 425.

discuss the abstract arguments for and against a policy which is rather at variance with that pursued to-day by several Colleges. One can only remark that it prevented the growth of a strong *esprit de corps*; but, on the other hand, diminished the chances that the many might exercise a tyranny over the unpopular and possibly impecunious minority. In Balliol it has had this lasting result, that the junior Common-room still plays a comparatively unimportant part in the life of the College, existing only as a voluntary association, and offering comparatively slight advantages to the members. Sconces, however, defied suppression, and are now so completely incorporated in the unwritten constitution, that the senior Fellow present at High Table is the recognised arbiter in all cases of dispute. Sconces, in fact, served a most necessary purpose in the eighteenth century, when the social amenities were more apt to be grossly and wilfully violated than they are with us. As a specimen of the witticisms which sconces served to suppress, we may quote one of which no less a person than Adam Smith was made the butt. At his first dinner in Hall he fell into a reverie, and utterly neglected his plate; whereupon his neighbour bade him wake up and fall to, adding that he could never in his life have had the chance of attacking such a joint as he now saw before him. The point of the jest thus aimed at a total stranger was that Adam Smith happened to be a Scotchman, and was therefore presumed to be poor. The modern undergraduate, when mulcted in a quart of beer for a pun or a quotation more than three words long, may solace himself by the reflection that the custom under which he suffers has at least done yeoman service in raising the standard of politeness and decorum.

[NOTE.—The *Terrae Filius* of 1733 thus apostrophises the Fellows of Balliol: "What sage instructors of Youth are you since by your extraordinary mulcts and fines you teach them the readiest and surest way to spend their money, and therefore it cannot be denied that if they improve nothing by you (which 'tis to be feared they don't much), yet you improve by them. . . . What Addition did you receive to your Fellowships last Year from sconcing and pinching poor Undergraduates? A man might think your House a Purgatory, since you take your Scholars' Money to pray for their souls. . . . You never frequent Chapel yourselves unless your office constrains you to it."]

CHAPTER XI

MODERN BALLIOL

Masters: Dr. Parsons, 1798; Dr. Jenkyns, 1819; Dr. Scott, 1854; Dr. Jowett, 1870.

No College in Oxford has parted with old traditions to the same extent as Balliol. The Commissions of 1854 and 1877 did much to impose a modern form upon all such foundations and reduce them, with few exceptions, to a superficial similarity. But the revolution which they made has not gone so far as might be supposed from the text of Ordinances and Statutes. The abolition of tests, the introduction of prize Fellows and married tutors, the redistribution of endowments, the stress laid upon free competition, are reforms which, though sweeping in themselves, by no means imply the disappearance of old ceremonies, habits, and prejudices. The peculiarity of Balliol has been that she welcomed, and indeed forestalled by some years, the main ideas of the Commissioners. Thus the Commissions merely accelerated the progress of the College along a self-chosen line, and are to be regarded as no more than accidents in the course of her development.

We do not wish to revive old controversies by discussing in detail each particular innovation through which the College advanced towards her ideal. She has lost some customs and some buildings which might well have been spared, if only for their associations. The lessons of the past have not always received a due consideration. But these errors concern us less than the general tendencies which have pervaded ninety years of change and movement. The question which is really vital to our purpose may be stated thus. These frequent innovations, some good and others of doubtful value, were they the outcome of a fixed policy, or do they represent the fitful activity of restless minds, shifting their point of view in response to every passing breeze of public opinion; and if so, what was that policy, and to what extent has it been successful?

To this question an answer of a kind can be readily given. Ever since the beginning of the century the first aim and object of the College has been to provide what is called a "liberal education." To this object all others have been subordinated, and it has never been called in question by any member of the governing body. At no time in this century has Balliol been the headquarters of a sect or a party. Learning, scholarship, criticism have always found a welcome there, but they have been welcomed less for their own sake than as instruments of education. More honour, perhaps, has been paid to philosophy, but even of the philosopher the demand has been made that he should justify his theories by proving them of value to the immature mind. It is not every College of which the same can be said; single-mindedness is no more usual in institutions than in individuals, and many errors may be forgiven to those who possess this fundamental virtue. But the nature of an aim is no less to be considered than the degree of tenacity with which it is pursued. And "education" is a wide term, admitting of very various interpretations. In what sense has it been understood by the great teachers who have made their home in Balliol? What were the ideas, and what was the attitude of mind which they sought to impress upon their pupils? These are the questions of which the present chapter may be reasonably expected to supply the answer.

But there is a preliminary objection of which some account must be taken. Balliol, it may be said, has produced in more recent times a number of men who have attained eminence in widely different spheres of activity. Of her alumni some have been scholars, critics, poets; others have sat in Parliaments or Cabinets, or have governed great dependencies; others have distinguished themselves in the learned professions on the comparatively narrow field of University life. But is it not idle to suppose that men so various in their tastes and pursuits are all equally indebted to the College within which they spent a few years on the way from school to a public or professional life? And even if they conform, in a way, to one general type may we not hold that they educated one another, and were really very little indebted to their seniors and ostensible teachers? These arguments are natural and they have a foundation in fact. In some degree every College is a democracy, and some of the conditions necessary to its success can only be realised by democratic means. Given a constant supply of brains and muscle and good humour, a broad similarity of preferences and prejudices, a reasonable respect for the past, and a reasonable readiness to sacrifice something for the sake of the future—with such an equipment a College may hold its own in social life and in the Schools, though it be weakly or even badly governed. But the intellectual life of a College is a more delicate plant than its public spirit or *morale*. At times there will be an exceptional coterie of men who instinctively turn to the best ideas, use the best methods, and set before themselves the highest standard of knowledge. But even they are apt to feel the need of a leader, more particularly when there is in the air a general spirit of undue scepticism or undue credulity. The nineteenth century has been prolific in these periods of exaltation and depression, and naturally enough their effects have been more keenly felt in Oxford than elsewhere. The task incumbent upon College tutors has been proportionately heavy wherever, as in Balliol, they have adequately realised their obligations. They have been called upon to cope with mental disease in all its most insidious forms. At first it was the shallow rationalism which we inherited from the eighteenth century; then came the fever and delirium of the Oxford Movement; then a period of exhaustion and apathy when the learner knew of no ideal as yet undemolished and no authority in whom he could place implicit trust. Against these dangers the keenest of minds, unaided and undisciplined, were wholly defenceless. They found themselves perilously near to the dilemma of Matthew Arnold:

"Is there no choice but this alone—
Madman or slave must man be one?"

The years 1830–70 cover a momentous crisis in the history of English thought. Our insular theology and metaphysics were cast into the fierce fire of Continental criticism; under this test, ideas which had been treasured as pure gold were exposed as dross and burnt away. There was urgent need of men who had the courage to face the results of destructive criticism and the power to inspire a like courage in others; still more of those who were sanguine enough to hope that a creed more comprehensive, more satisfying than the old, was still within the range of possibility. Fortunately for Balliol she possessed such men at the time when they were most needed; and this is the secret of her practical success. The first lesson which they have taught has always been this: that men are greater than theories, that practice is the end of life, and that all practice must be grounded on the faith which is innate in the human mind; the second, that this faith is not bound up with the dogmas of any sect, and in no way depends upon the truth of so-called historic facts; the third, that, within the limits prescribed by faith, reason is the only trustworthy guide.

It is in this teaching much more than in the fortuitous intercourse of gifted and inquiring spirits that we find the origin of a mental attitude which was at first acknowledged by friends and enemies as peculiar to Balliol, but now tends more and more to be characteristic of Oxford men at large. Whatever may be thought of that attitude, the Balliol system, to which it is due, claims our respect as the fruit of much unostentatious self-sacrifice and much thankless labour. The men who made the system knew well what they were doing, and counted no price too high to pay for success. They did not take the pose of oracles or prophets. They did not become teachers in the belief that this was the highest of all professions, or that in which they were most likely to make a reputation. They taught because they had ideas to impart, and this was the most obvious opportunity of imparting them; because the College had need of them, and they knew what a power the College might become. It was something more than a jest when Jowett confessed his desire "to inoculate the world with Balliol." For this end he and his colleagues were prepared to give every available hour of their time, to renounce fair hopes of literary reputation, and to spend the whole of the scanty emoluments which were their rightful due. We may fairly apply to them all the words of the epitaph which was written for the youngest of them:* "He loved great things and thought little of himself. Desiring neither fame nor influence he won the love of men and was a power in their lives; and seeking no disciples he taught to many the greatness of the world and of man's mind." The results of a work pursued in this spirit at least deserve our sympathetic consideration. And the nature of the work is best understood by passing in review the successive waves of doubt and difficulty to which the rising generations of 1830-70 were exposed, by taking into account the dangers against which these teachers sought to fortify their pupils. We shall then be more in a position to appreciate the frame of mind which they endeavoured to form.

On a certain June morning of 1794 Fisher's Buildings witnessed an interview which may be regarded as in some degree forecasting the fortunes of Balliol in the

* R. L. Nettleship. From the tablet in the College Chapel.

next hundred years. Coleridge, the father of English idealism, the first writer to turn the attention of Englishmen upon that new movement of thought which Kant had originated, was brought by a bookseller to call on Robert Southey, the typical Englishman of talent, bubbling over with wild theories and enthusiasms, but also a true conservative by temperament, and endowed with just so much enthusiasm as would enable him, when the hot blood of youth had subsided, to appreciate the charm and the worth of the existing order of things. For such a man could any friend seem less desirable than a heterodox, unpractical mystic such as Coleridge? And yet in the end both were gainers by the meeting. Southey obtained from Coleridge ideas of more lasting value than any which he was likely to find in the course of aimless rebellions against convention and uncritical prostrations before the altar of Rousseau. Coleridge, too, learned a lesson of which he stood in need.

"I dwell," he says, "with unabated pleasure on the strong and sudden, but I trust not fleeting, influence which my moral being underwent on my acquaintance with him (*i.e.*, Southey) at Oxford. The irregularities only not universal among the young men of my standing, which I always knew to be wrong, I then learned to feel as degrading; learned to know that an opposite conduct which was at that time considered by us as the easy virtue of a cold and selfish prudence, might originate in the noblest emotions, in views the most disinterested and imaginative."

The two opposite poles of the English character—the speculative and the practical—had been brought into contact, and nothing but good had resulted from the shock. The first visit of Coleridge to Balliol was also his last; but the object of the Balliol system has always been to impress upon minds such as Southey's the thought of Coleridge and his great fellow worker Wordsworth.

The Balliol to which Coleridge came was still, in the main, unregenerate. Some reforms, indeed, had taken place, but they were narrow and of a piecemeal character. In 1776 a Fellowship was, with the Visitor's consent, temporarily suppressed;* in 1789 a regular building fund was created; and with the funds thus obtained Wyatt was set to work upon the front Quadrangle (1794). The Library was restored with tolerable skill; the Hall was transformed into a modern room, more comfortable if less picturesque than it had been before; the Master's house was rebuilt, and the entrance to the back Quadrangle was removed from the south to the north end of the Hall. In 1802 it was resolved to set apart, for purposes of a similar nature, a portion of the revenues which were just beginning to arise from the mines on the Stamfordham property. It had taken the Fellows some years to decide in favour of a sacrifice so reasonable and so necessary. There were two parties among them, of which one desired to restore the whole fabric in the " Grecian " style, concealing with façades and friezes and pilasters the negligent irregularity which was the greatest charm of the old buildings,† while the other objected to any scheme whatever which would impair the Fellowship dividend. Ultimately the party of progress triumphed. They were happily dissuaded from their more ambitious architectural designs, but on

---

* It was restored in 1816.
† Skelton, *Oxonia Illustrata*, Plate 45.

the death of Dr. Davey they carried the election to the Mastership, and in doing so inaugurated an era of far less questionable improvements. Their candidate was Dr. Parsons, and he was elected in 1798, four years after Coleridge's visit.

A Tory of the Tories, a staunch foe to Catholic emancipation, and one of Lord Eldon's bishops,* Dr. Parsons was hardly the man from whom sweeping changes might be hoped or feared. But in academic matters he was a consistent Liberal. Personal feeling may have had something to do with this attitude. Nineteen years before his election to the Mastership he had competed for a Balliol Fellowship, and had sustained an unexpected and undeserved repulse from the party of reaction, who, while acknowledging the great merit of his papers, flatly refused to vote for an outsider.† He may, therefore, have found a little natural pleasure in dealing the *coup de grâce* to a policy from which he himself had suffered. But, according to his lights, he was sincerely devoted to the cause of education. Already the interest of the Fellows in Scholarships was reviving; Nichols tells us that some of them had resolved to combine in editing a Latin dictionary; but the Master persuaded them to turn their energies to the work of teaching. There was now a regular scheme of College lectures—too regular to please independent minds like Hamilton. To the unbounded disgust of the undergraduate, an Entrance Examination was instituted, and the ordeal of "Collections" became

* Bishop of Peterborough, 1813.
† Parsons was a Scholar, and after his rejection at Balliol, a Fellow of Wadham.

a terminal event. The zeal of Dr. Parsons was not bounded by the walls of his own College. In conjunction with Dr. Eveleigh of Oriel he accepted the duty of framing new Examination Statutes for the University. The object of the change was to give able men a more arduous test than that of the ordinary Pass Examination. But even Parsons did not venture to make the Honours Examination obligatory for Balliol men; and, to tell the truth, they failed for some time to avail themselves of the new opportunity for distinction. Balliol obtained no first-class in mathematics till 1808, nor in Literae Humaniores until 1810. It was not before 1820 that it became a matter of course to find the names of Balliol men at the head of the list, and there was no case of a Double-First from the College until 1820.

Of Dr. Parsons there is little more to be said, except that he was an active Vice-Chancellor, a prominent member of the Athenæum, and co-founder with Joshua Watson of the once famous National Schools Society. An antithetical obituary notice tells us that he hated flattery and never asked for preferment; that he preached good sermons, but declined to print them; that, while in general society he wore an air of serious reserve, his conversation among intimate friends sparkled with "lively narrative, unstudied wit, playful and inoffensive gaiety"; that "the entire line of his progress was marked by a series of improvements, of institutions reformed, of revenues augmented, of residences restored and embellished." On his death in 1819 he was succeeded by Dr. Jenkyns, who for the last six years had been Vice-gerent during the repeated absences of the Bishop from the College.

The election was likely to surprise those who had but a slight acquaintance with the new Master. Dr. Jenkyns had won his Scholarship and Fellowship at a time when there was comparatively little competition for these prizes. His intellect was in no way remarkable; though his will was strong, his personality could hardly be called commanding. In appearance he was neat and insignificant. His formal manners, his mincing speech, his comical gait, and his little white pony formed the subject of many ludicrous legends. As for his convictions, he was a high-and-dry Churchman of the old school, scrupulously orthodox, bitterly opposed to what he called the " superstitions " of the Tractarians, and entirely unable to see why a man should not be content with the beliefs which had been good enough for the generation of Dr. Parsons. Sympathy, in fact, was the last thing to be expected from him. He had a narrow pattern of deportment with which he expected all his " young men " to conform; and deep in his heart there lurked a conviction that, except by a special providence, no boy could become a gentleman if he had not been through one of two or three great public schools. During his tenure of office the majority of the commoners of the College were carefully chosen from Eton, Rugby and Harrow. But his attempts at friendly intercourse with this select coterie were almost always laughable. He was courteous and kindly, but he could not meet them either as a mentor or as a friend. One day, when preaching in Chapel, he announced as his text "The sin that doth so easily beset us"; "and by this," he began, "I mean the habit of contracting debts." The unconscious bathos, and the emphatic acidity of the Master's tone, were irresistible; for the first and last time in its history the College Chapel resounded with Homeric laughter. One of Jenkyns' pupils used to describe with much humour how, on a winter morning after Chapel, the Master sent for him and said, with a trace of asperity, "I hear, Mr. Rogers, that you sing." The charge was modestly admitted. "I hear, Mr. Rogers, that you are a good singer." Mr. Rogers replied that his friends were sometimes pleased to say as much. "You sing a song called 'Jolly Nose,' Mr. Rogers!" This, too, was undeniable. "Sing it now, Mr. Rogers!" There was no way of escape; the song had to be sung before the vocalist was dismissed to his breakfast; but the purpose of this odd invitation was never divulged.*

Beneath this superficial eccentricity there lay some valuable qualities. Dr. Jenkyns was, to use the phrase of Dean Church, "an unfailing judge of a clever man as a jockey might be of a horse." Under his auspices the Fellowship elections were marked by the highest discrimination, and tutorial work was entrusted to the very pick of the Fellows. Nor was this all. Jowett himself hardly possessed a more truly magnanimous disposition than Dr. Jenkyns. The old man's opinions were clear-cut, but he quite realised that a rigid uniformity could only be obtained by sacrificing the best interests of the College. He carried the principle of tolerance to the farthest limits consistent with the obligations of his position. He would sacrifice his most darling prejudices to give a good teacher free scope.

* A rather different version is given in the *Reminiscences of the Rev. W. Rogers*. But we give that in the text on oral authority.

He felt that no teacher could well be spared, however startling the propositions of which he was the mouthpiece, so long as his moral influence with "the young men" was obviously good. Probably he had never read a line of Milton's *Areopagitica;* but his idea of a healthy intellectual society might have been taken directly from that immortal pamphlet. Almost equally remarkable was the tact with which he kept the peace among his Fellows. He conciliated the younger men by the good grace with which he submitted to reforms concerning the expediency of which he had the gravest doubts. In 1828 he allowed the Scholarships to be thrown open to free competition, not because he expected any good from the change, but because the tutors were unanimous on the other side. In 1839 he assented to a decree which enabled Fellowships to be conferred on those who had no intention of taking orders, subject, of course, to the condition that the Fellowship must be vacated when the statutory time of grace had expired. Nothing was less to his liking than a measure which seemed to advertise Balliol as a refuge for the heretic and the Arnoldian; but he bowed to the consensus of the majority. On the other hand, he appeased the conservatives by choosing for his prime ministers such men as Ogilvie, Tait, and Woollcombe, who were personally acceptable to all parties in the Common Room.

Near as they seem to our own day, the thirties are already ancient history. The manners and thoughts of Oxford have changed incredibly since then. We must picture to ourselves a community which dined at four in the afternoon, read or was supposed to read without a break from morning-chapel to dinner time, and took its exercise in the early evening. The hour between five and six was usually spent at a wine-party. After this function the company dispersed, some to walk out in pairs for a constitutional, others to the river. Rowing had lately come into fashion; an eight was put upon the river for the first time about 1835; already the College was roughly divided into rowing and non-rowing men. The Master long refused to believe that rowing was an amusement for gentlemen. But when at last, by an ingenious stratagem, he was brought down to Sandford, and saw the eight go by at a racing stroke, he was instantly converted. "It is like the motion of one man!" he cried, and rode back to the College beaming with delight. Other forms of athletics were not much in vogue. Football was unknown and cricket very little played. Some found their recreation in the weekly debates of the Union. Manning, who entered Balliol in 1828, soon became conspicuous among the first generation of Union orators; his more active exercise was taken in the form of boxing lessons. In one way and another the hours between six and nine were devoted to recreation. Then came supper, with perhaps a little reading to follow. But the usual hour for bed was half-past ten.

Old ideas were as deeply engrained as old ways of life. This was particularly the case in the Senior Common Room, where a clerical atmosphere necessarily prevailed. All the serious talk was of theology. The seniors held by Butler and Barrow; the juniors were divided in their allegiance between Arnold and Newman. Controversy began to grow hot about the year 1827, when Frederic Oakeley was elected a Fellow; and so great was the chagrin of the older generation that they fled from arguments which they could not refute, and ostentatiously absented themselves from the after-dinner circle. But this preliminary ferment was as nothing compared with that produced by the entry of W. G. Ward (1834). Both Ward and Oakeley were disciples of Newman. The older man was led by æsthetic instincts which revolted from the dry logic and the colourless ritual of the older Anglicanism. Ward's was a more complex and powerful intellect. An acute mathematician, with little liking for any art but music, and even less respect for the past, he had an unrivalled faculty of arguing from given premisses, and a reckless resolution "to go whithersoever the argument should lead him." Unfortunately he was contented to take his premisses on trust from Newman. It was his strong and his weak point that he entertained an intense but somewhat indiscriminating reverence for moral elevation of character. Having chosen his leaders on this ground, he deferred to them even in questions where moral qualities were a very insufficient guide. For such a mind in such a time there could be only one destiny; his friends were aware, long before himself, that Rome would be his ultimate port of refuge.

In spite of this weakness—which, in fact, was only developed by degrees—Ward was for some years the chief intellectual force in the College. If he rushed headlong into every quarrel, it seemed to be less from the gladiator's love of fighting than from a sincere interest in all questions that, however remotely, concerned human welfare. Uncouth in appearance, negligent in dress, boisterous in demeanour, always full of some new paradox and shifting his views with kaleidoscopic rapidity, he had still an irresistible fascination for younger men. He seemed to them, before he stood declared as a partisan, "a kind of Silenus-Socrates," born to sift the opinions of others and force them to think for themselves. No influence could stand against his, not even that of Tait, who had been elected in the same year with himself. Tait was clear, incisive, and full of common sense, but there was neither method nor imagination in his teaching. He hated abstractions, he had no counter-system to oppose to that of Newman and Ward, and he was totally unable to appreciate an opponent's point of view. His character commanded more respect than his views; and if in the Common Room his battles with Ward were fairly drawn, outside it there was no comparison between the followings of the two.

The retirement of Oakeley from the College, followed as it was by his conversion to Romanism, weakened the party of the new theology both in numbers and in prestige. Ward's opinions were rapidly crystallising, and their tendency could no longer be doubted. He was now no Socrates but a sophist. He was trying to make converts when he ought to have been teaching mathematics. His pupils, confronted with the imperious dilemma, "Believe in nothing or believe in the one true Church!" felt themselves, as Clough once confessed, "like pieces of paper sucked up a chimney." To prove his case Ward sapped their faith in all methods of proof. To induce credulity he drove them headlong into a desperate scepticism. The question was no longer concerning the orthodoxy of Ward's theories of the Ideal Church. He was palpably unhinging the minds and ruining the characters of those whom he influenced. Tait, therefore, though still on friendly terms with his rival, persuaded the Master to ask that Ward should resign his tutorial work (1841). It was an extreme step, but the danger, too, was extreme. Ward himself acknowledged that the Master, from his point of view, was acting with perfect justice and propriety. Dr. Jenkyns, on his side, was sincerely sorry for the pass to which Ward had brought himself. He shed tears at their final interview, and was afterwards overheard in his garden murmuring to himself in an agitated undertone: "I wish Mrs. Jenkyns would take care of the flowers instead of the cabbages," and immediately afterward, "I wish Mr. Ward would not write such pamphlets."

Ward retained his Fellowship, and kept a party together until 1846. His marriage and his subsequent change of communion did much to break the spell of his ascendency. But he had set in motion an agitation which was independent of his personality. For some years after 1841 the best minds of the College seemed to be smitten with a kind of paralysis. They had lost their most fundamental convictions, and had found nothing with which to replace them. They had been plunged in a labyrinth of vexed questions without the semblance of a clue. They had lost all interest in their prescribed pursuits, and had no heart to strike out others for themselves. Their unfortunate position has been most graphically described by Clough and Matthew Arnold, who were themselves among the sufferers. It is a small fact, but worthy of notice in this connection, that both took Seconds in the Schools, and that in the years 1841-44 Balliol obtained no more than three Firsts altogether.

With such a disease of the intellect Jenkyns was quite unable to deal, the more so since in 1842 he lost the assistance of Tait, who was called away from Oxford to Rugby. There was need of a younger man who had himself felt the crisis, and who had won his own battle before he was called upon to arm others for it. Such a man the College found in Jowett. He had been elected to a Fellowship in 1838; he succeeded to a tutorship in 1842, directly after Tait's retirement; and, in spite of his youth, he became almost immediately the mainstay of the tutorial body.

Jowett was not at this time a "philosopher" in the ordinary sense of the word. He was hardly acquainted, that is, with German speculations, and he had hardly yet begun those appreciative studies of Greek thought for which he was afterwards to be famous. He had been half inclined to think Ward a martyr, and he had not yet decided for or against the Tractarians. But he intended to decide for himself and at leisure. "I had resolved," he said afterwards, "to read through the Fathers, and if I found Puseyism there, to become a Puseyite." There was little danger for such a spirit. His almost preternatural sagacity at once thrust the systems of Ward and such thinkers into their proper historical perspective. He saw that the questions to be solved were deeper than most of his contemporaries suspected. He saw, too, that these questions could not be handled except after an arduous preliminary training of the critical faculty. He began simultaneously to train himself and to train others.

This is not the place to describe how for the next fourteen or fifteen years his mind wandered from Plato to St. John, from Hegel to Comte. He read widely and encouraged his pupils to do the same; but eclecticism was the last result at which he aimed. He learned something from every philosopher, but he was never a mere borrower. Experience, he said in effect, is our one clue to the nature of man, the world and God. But in the interpretation of personal experience we must call to our aid the great minds of the past; they will help us to analyse what we have thought and felt. As our experience is ever growing wider, so must we always be adding to our knowledge. For that reason a final system can never be constructed; at the best a system is but a synthesis of what we know in the present state of our experience. He who adopts a system closes the eyes of the mind; he becomes blind to the facts which controvert his theory. Of final truth no man can have more than glimpses; but every man who is honest with himself finds in his own nature so much of the truth as suffices for the practical conduct of life. The essential doctrines of Christianity are in fact proved by experience; they do not stand or fall with historic documents. They may be supplemented from those documents, but of this we cannot be certain until those documents have been more critically examined and interpreted in a more impartially historic spirit.

Such was the position to which his mind was driven. The practical result upon his teaching was to make him the great populariser of Hellenic thought. In the Greek poets and philosophers he saw revealed every stage of development through which the human consciousness has passed. There were few conceivable experiences of the human mind which were not subjected to examination by these writers. And, since they approached their subject with untrammelled minds, no guides could be more suitable for those whom he desired to turn their backs upon the clouds and dust of modern controversy, and to form their opinions on the basis of first principles. Of all the Greeks, Plato pleased him the most. There was, he said, no question which Plato had not handled; no thinker had more of the true prophetic imagination; none was more free from the vice of system-building. And this is why Jowett sacrificed the leisure of his best years to the thankless task of translating the Dialogues. He wished to make accessible to the world the panacea of which Matthew Arnold had already proclaimed the sovereign efficacy.

Much good work was done in Balliol between 1840 and 1870. The scholarship of the College had never reached a higher level than it now reached under the care of such men as Edwin Palmer and James Riddell. Increased attention was paid to mathematics, for the College had secured the services of Henry Smith. History and political science received a more careful attention; there are many who can still attest the profound impression which was made upon them by the lectures which Mr. W. L. Newman delivered on these subjects. But to mention names is almost invidious. The tutors of Balliol in those years were the *élite* of the University, and thought no sacrifice of time or labour too great for the sake of their pupils. It was no uncommon thing for them to hear essays and correct compositions in the small hours of the morning. Even their vacations brought no rest; if they travelled it was to gather new ideas for their lectures; and reading-parties were constantly formed so that backward pupils might be raised to the necessary standard. In his own department each was unrivalled; but Jowett was the guiding spirit of all, and though his influence was exposed to checks of many kinds, he was on the whole successful in subordinating every department of tuition to the object which he had in view.

This is hardly the place to speak in detail of the differences which were occasionally inevitable between men of powerful minds and strong characters, who differed in so many respects that they often seemed to have no other tie than that of a common patriotism. It is enough to say that Dr. Jenkyns, though keenly alive to the great services of Jowett and aware that his moral influence on the "young men" was most admirable, took fright in the last years of his life. He thought that his junior was moving too fast; he thought his teaching not only inconsistent with Anglican doctrines, but inconsistent with Christianity. This suspicion was not without effect upon the Fellowship elections; and, when Jenkyns died in 1854, the majority of the electors refused to have Jowett. Scott, who had been, some fifteen or sixteen years before, a prominent tutor of the College, was recalled from his College living to the vacant Mastership; for ten years it was impossible for Jowett to make those changes in the discipline and teaching system which he deemed essential to the success of his plans; and there was a breach in the friendly relations of the two parties, which only extreme forbearance and self-control upon both sides prevented from damaging the efficiency of the College. At one time a wave of reaction was feared. The majority passed a decree for compelling the Scholars to subscribe to the doctrines of the Church of England; it was whispered that Jowett would be driven out of his tutorship. But the ill-advised decree was vetoed by a Visitor, whose impartiality could not be called in question; and those who prophesied that the Master and his friends would resort to extreme measures against their opponents did less than justice to the real generosity and breadth of mind which lay beneath the crust of fixed opinions. This unfortunate period led to no worse result than the removal of the old Chapel. The object, to raise a memorial to Dr. Jenkyns, was one in which all could sympathise; and the new building, designed by Butterfield, has a certain beauty of its own. But there were many who wished that the founder of the new Balliol had been commemorated in any other way, and Jowett was of this number.

After 1864 the deadlock came to an end. A single Fellowship election turned the scale in Jowett's favour. Thenceforth to the day of his death there was no question of his supremacy. His ideal was now thoroughly formed, and so, too, was the method through which he thought it could be realised. When, six years later, he was at length elected to the Mastership (1870) he could afford to leave routine work in the hands of younger men. He never neglected the duty, to which he was bound by the Statutes, of participating in the tutorial work. He took the keenest interest in the weekly conclaves, instituted by himself, at which the work and conduct of every individual undergraduate were passed in review. The sensations with which the freshmen carried their first essay to his study are vividly remembered by those who entered the College so late as 1890. But then, and indeed for some time before then, the ordeal had become more of an inspection than a lesson. Rebuke or praise was given in a few emphatic words; suggestions and explanations came but rarely. The consciousness that he distinguished good work from bad at a glance was an immense incentive. His verdict was accepted as irreversible. But it was no longer his part to show how the work should be done, any more than it is the duty of a general to drill the rank and file.

The machine which he had made continued to work with unabated vigour. And enough has now been said to show why it could influence and develop minds of the most various casts. The matter of Jowett's curriculum was mainly the philosophy and the literature of ancient Greece; the spirit of it was critical; the aim proposed was to excite the love of truth and to stimulate sound methods of reflection. Hence he taught some to analyse the theory of art, others to be metaphysicians, others to explore the thoughts and the springs of action of the past; while of others again he made debaters and statesmen. Some were more influenced by the subjects to which he directed their attention; some carried away with them little more than an appreciation of the subtle, cautious, inquiring attitude of mind which he exemplified. But he had something to teach every one; and no man ever had a more devoted band of followers.*

It has been said that Jowett's teaching was too negative. To this criticism there are two answers. He held that the only results of value are those which a man reaches for himself. Truth cannot be seen with the eyes of another; the most that a teacher can do is to indicate the road which leads to the vision. He had his own beliefs and held them fast; but he knew that no good would come of dictating them into note-books. Perhaps he put this view of the case too strongly; but the truth involved in his position has been more or less recognised by all great educators from the days of Socrates downward. And, again, his exaggeration of this truth must be explained by reference to the raw material on which he had to work in the years when his theory was forming. The freshman of the thirties and forties, to whatever cause we may ascribe the fact, was a more mature being than his counterpart of to-day. He was, perhaps, not so fine a scholar, nor even so erudite, but, if any faith may be placed in memoirs and

---

* The following list, though imperfect, of Jowett's more distinguished pupils may be of interest. It is mainly compiled from the *Life*, by Campbell and Abbott: W. R. Anson, H. H. Asquith, A. C. Bradley, W. St. John Brodrick, L. Campbell, E. Caird, G. N. Curzon, Earl of Elgin, J. A. Godley, A. Grant, T. H. Green, C. B. Heberden, C. P. Ilbert, F. H. Jeune, W. P. Ker, A. Lang, R. Lodge, K. M. Mackenzie, W. H. Mallock, A. Milner, R. B. D. Morier, W. W. Merry, R. L. Nettleship, W. L. Newman, J. Nichol, F. T. Palgrave, A. W. Peel, T. Raleigh, W. G. Rutherford, D. G. Ritchie, W. Y. Sellar, J. C. Shairp, H. Smith, A. Swinburne, J. A. Symonds, A. Toynbee, T. Walrond, W. Wallace, J. C. Wilson, T. H. Warren.

biographies, he had more ideas on things in general. The fear was, less that he would be left without a creed, than that he would come to man's estate with a jumble of strong but mutually inconsistent convictions. Even scepticism was in him the outcome of fire and fury. The work of a tutor in that age was much more to clarify ideas than to impart them. Jowett was accustomed to say, towards the end of his life, that he missed in the rising generation the enthusiasm which had characterised his own contemporaries. The time for revising his method to suit new conditions had long since passed. But fortunately that method was, for some years before and after his accession to the Mastership, supplemented, and in a measure counteracted, by the rival methods of Arnold Toynbee and T. H. Green.

Toynbee joined the teaching-staff in 1866, and remained on it until his untimely death in 1883. Though he was appointed ostensibly to lecture to the Indian Civilians, of whom there were then considerable numbers in the College, his influence reached far beyond that narrow circle. The vigour and acuteness with which he criticised the older political economy gained for him a ready hearing from all who were interested in the practical problems of modern government. No man was ever more thoroughly permeated with Jowett's belief that education must aim at preparing men for a life of action; but his teaching was rendered more, rather than less, effective by enthusiasm of a kind which was almost foreign to the Master's nature. He died at the moment when a remarkable career seemed to be opening before him; but the most characteristic ideas of his teaching have outlived him; and his memory is perpetuated by Toynbee Hall, which was established shortly after his death in Whitechapel, and was, from the very first, supported in great measure by the contributions of Balliol men. Toynbee Hall was to realise a dream, which Toynbee had shared with Jowett and several more among his colleagues, of promoting closer and more cordial relations between working men and those educated in Universities. Lectures were to be delivered and classes held, but the greatest benefit expected was the diminution of those class-prejudices which are chiefly the result of ignorance on both sides. In the estrangement of class from class Toynbee, like others before and since, saw the great danger for modern civilisation.

But Toynbee himself was in many respects the pupil of T. H. Green, whose influence, though less obvious in his own day than that of his more brilliant junior, has been at least as far-reaching. Green became a Fellow in 1862, a Tutor in 1866; after Jowett's election he at once became the right-hand man of the new Master. Their speculative differences never chilled the warmth of their intimacy. These differences were, however, great; for Green was, above all things, a system-builder, and, for that reason, the magnetic influence which he exercised both over his own pupils and over those with whom his contact was but casual, caused Jowett some hours of uneasiness. But Green gave ideas to men who were scantily provided with them, and, what was more important, set an example of high purpose, of connected and laborious thought, of confidence in the powers of the human reason, which was invaluable even to those who could not go far with him in his own peculiar speculations. Some took a creed from him, to others he indicated a starting-point for independent reflection. There were those who foreboded that Green's favourite studies would have a narrowing effect upon the intellectual interests of the College, and shook their heads over a fancied decline in the standards of taste and scholarship. But results, both in the Schools and in wider arenas, have gone far to show that these fears were tinged with exaggeration. There are many who still think that no better place of education can be imagined than one in which the "Credo" of Green should be constantly opposed to the "Quæro" of Jowett. Of the teachers whom Balliol has lost in comparatively recent times there was none more justly prized than R. L. Nettleship, in whom the two conflicting tendencies seem to have found the justest equilibrium.

But enough has been said of merely intellectual matters. There was no man who hated, more than Jowett, the doctrine, so dear to the English middle-class, that only those virtues are worth the cultivation which make no demand upon the intellectual faculties; but he would have been the last to admit that a College is no more than a workshop. Of the practical improvements which he undertook, both as Tutor and as Master, many, of course, related to the severer occupations of his pupils. Much thought, for example, was devoted to the formation of the Undergraduates' Library, to the foundation of new scholarships and exhibitions, to enlarging the range of studies, to providing accommodation for Indian civilians and artisan-undergraduates. But Jowett was at least as much concerned to make the

College a pleasant and commodious centre of social intercourse. He knew that cliques and sets must exist, but he hoped to make them less exclusive by providing new opportunities for general reunions, and by encouraging those pursuits in which all had a common interest. His devices for throwing men together were sometimes more ingenious than successful. The average undergraduate who goes on Saturday morning, only half awake, and shivering in a costume more remarkable for simplicity than elegance, to receive his Battells from the butler in the presence of the Master, seldom realises that he has been brought there to improve his acquaintanceship with all sorts and conditions of his fellows. Yet we have been assured on good authority that this was one among several reasons which the late Master gave for the innovation of a weekly "Battell-call." But this is hardly a fair instance. The Master was much more successful in other plans inspired by the same general purpose. The College owes to him the handsome block of buildings, comprising a Hall, a Common Room, Buttery, and Kitchen, which to-day forms the background of the Garden Quadrangle. No other influence than Jowett's would have been sufficient to raise the large sum required for this scheme. The new buildings were not an absolute necessity, for already, in Scott's Mastership, the more pressing requirements of space had been satisfied; the east and south sides of the front Quadrangle had been rebuilt on a larger scale,* partly at the expense of Miss Brackenbury, the most munificent of our modern benefactors, partly by the sacrifice of dividends. But the Hall and

---

* After designs by Waterhouse.

From a Photograph by the] [Oxford Camera Club

THE NEW HALL

the Common Room were needed for gatherings of many kinds, and the Master, who firmly believed in good living as an ingredient of good-fellowship, hoped that the College cooks would be fired to prove themselves worthy of their new quarters. He had an equal belief in the virtue of good music. The organs which are to be seen in the Hall and the Chapel were a gift from his private purse. That in the Hall was, of course, intended for concerts. Even before it was set up, concerts had become a regular institution of the College. At first they were given on Saturday afternoons, under the auspices of the present Principal of Brasenose. But in 1885 Mr. John Farmer came from Harrow, at the Master's invitation, to take up the duties of organist and Kapellmeister; and, immediately afterwards the Musical Society was induced to begin that series of Sunday evening concerts for which Balliol has become famous in Oxford.

The interest which Jowett took in the athletics of the College is attested by the new Cricket Ground, than which there is no better in Oxford. It was not acquired before 1890, but for years it had been the pet project of the Master; he had thought of it as early as 1852. Rowing, too, claimed his sympathies; and the adventures of the Eight were watched by him with hardly less anxiety than the class-lists of the Schools.

Perhaps the class-lists were more uniformly satisfactory than the results obtained upon the river and in the cricket-field. But, in justice to the College clubs, it must be remarked that for more than thirty years an Honours School has been compulsory for every Balliol undergraduate. Consequently the Eight and the

Eleven are not to be judged by the same standard as those of Colleges where larger sacrifices are made to athletic prestige. Still the record of both is gratifying. The eight-oar summer races began in 1836; Balliol was one of the first Colleges to join in them, and in fifteen years from that time her Eight had become one of the best upon the river. It finished as head boat in 1851, in 1855, and again in 1859–60. These successes were followed by a short period of depression; but the crews of 1873 and 1879 fully repaired the reputation of the College. For the last twenty years the Eight has failed to regain the coveted position, but it has been more than once within an ace of doing so, and of late years has uniformly held an excellent position. In 1890 and 1891 it carried off the Ladies' Plate at Henley, and in 1899 enjoyed the almost unique privilege of furnishing five oars to the crew which represented Oxford in the race of the year. In all, since 1864, the College has produced a dozen rowing Blues. Her representatives at Lord's have been less numerous, but an Eleven which, in comparatively recent times, has produced such batsmen as A. K. L. H. Watson and M. Jardine, and such bowlers as J. B. Wood and P. Waddy, has no cause to be ashamed.

As for class-lists and such honours, are they not to be read in the University Calendar? Those, however, who care for statistics may be pleased to know that, from 1830 to the present time, there has been only one break in the continuous series of Firsts. This break, on the reason of which we have already touched, occurred in the years 1841–44. Since then the College successes, both in Literae Humaniores and in younger Schools, have shown a constant tendency to increase in numbers. Again, out of the sixty Ireland Scholarships awarded in the years 1837-96, Balliol has won no less than thirty-four; and, in the same period, the Hertford has fallen an almost equal number of times to members of the College.

But these figures have brought us to the verge of times which as yet need no historian. It only remains to close a book which has exceeded all due limits of length with the wish that the College founded for the first time by John and Dervorguilla de Balliol, and practically refounded by Parsons, Jenkyns, and Jowett, may never lack a constant succession of such benefactors and such rulers. For a century past Balliol men have been less accustomed to contemplate the past than the future. The tendency is justifiable, for the last chapter in the history of the College has been by far the most glorious, and there is no reason to fear that the last page of it will be turned for many years to come. Still the present owes much to the immediate and something also to the remoter past. If these truths have been emphasised by our history, its purpose will have been fully served.

APPENDICES

I.—AUTHORITIES FOR THE COLLEGE HISTORY

A.—Previous Histories.

Balliofergus, by Henry Savage. This is an attempt to tell the history of the College from the documents of the archives. It contains, moreover, some account of the buildings, and notes on the lives of eminent Balliol men. Savage was assisted in the work by Anthony Wood, who lent him some notes. The book is badly arranged, and is not free from errors, even where it adheres most closely to the documents; but contains much useful information, particularly on the seventeenth century.

Early History of Balliol College, by the Baroness de Paravicini. Deals with the period anterior to 1600, and chiefly with the thirteenth and fourteenth centuries. It contains a number of most useful transcripts from the Wood MSS., the College register, and the archives.

Balliol College, by Mr. R. L. Poole, in Clark's *Colleges of Oxford,* leaves little more to be said on the fourteenth and fifteenth centuries; but, owing to the scope of the book in which it is included, passes somewhat hastily over the later history. Contains a most valuable account of the Renaissance movement.

Sketches of the College history are to be found in

APPENDICES

Woods' *Colleges and Halls*, Pointer's *Oxoniensis Academia*, Ayliffe's *University of Oxford*, Chalmers' *Oxford* (1810), Ingram's *Memorials of Oxford*, Wells' *Oxford Colleges*. The foundation and original constitution are discussed by Mr. Rashdall, *Universities*, vol. ii., part ii. His sketch is valuable for the references to the Lincoln register which it contains. Mr. Maxwell Lyte, in his *University of Oxford*, has given some useful references respecting John of Balliol.

B.—MSS. MATERIAL.

(1) In the College.

The deeds in the archives have been admirably arranged, catalogued, and indexed by Mr. Parker. The hand-list (MS.) prepared by him is kept in the Bursary. With its help the student will have no difficulty in tracing the documents used in our pages. The bulk of the deeds refer to the endowments and estates. The correspondence of the College with its Visitors has been preserved with more or less irregularity since 1700, and is to be found here. A printed account of the more interesting deeds is given by Mr. Riley in the Fourth Report of the Historical Manuscripts Commission.

The *College Register*, now kept in the Old Library, contains a few scattered entries from 1514 to 1538. In 1538 a secretary was appointed to keep the minutes of Fellows' meetings; thenceforth the entries are fairly regular. The information given is chiefly of a formal character: *e.g.*, the elections to Fellowships, offices, scholarships, and exhibitions; the assignment of rooms, new by-laws, reprimands administered at College meetings. A number of leases and letters are transcribed or bound up into the *Register*. Very little information as to the critical periods of the College history is to be derived either from the Register or from the Bursar's Books, which begin in 1545. The Register during the Parliamentary Visitation is content to give the Visitors' decrees. The accounts for the same period are kept with great irregularity. The most valuable material contained in these volumes was collected by Dr. Wall, a recent Bursar of the College. He compiled : (1) A chronological list of Fellows, Masters and Visitors since 1520; (2) a catalogue of benefactions from the foundation down to 1864.* The latter must be supplemented from the three volumes in the Old Library, which give : (1) A list of Fellow-Commoners, 1649–1717 (imperfect) and their donations ; (2) a list of benefactors to the Chapel from 1636 onwards; (3) a list of books given to the Library and their donors (breaks off early in the eighteenth century).

Some further information can be obtained from the *Catalogue of Exhibitions*, the Master's copy of the *Statutes*, and the early *Admission Books* (from about 1635), all of which are kept in the Old Library.

(2) In the Bodleian Library.

Mr. Madan's Catalogue of MSS. relating to the various Colleges in the University appears to be complete, so far as Balliol is concerned. The following papers are worthy of notice :

Rawlinson MSS. B. 376, fol. 49, 156–9. Letters to and from Bishop Robinson, the Visitor, concerning a Blundell Scholar (1718–19).

Tanner MSS. 338, *fol.* 227 *seqq.* Letters relating to the Warner Exhibitions (1680) from the Warner trustees.

Rawlinson MSS. 810 *D. fol.* 35. This volume is the commonplace book of Hannibal Baskerville of Sunningwell, a contemporary of Wood and Savage. He gives a number

* Both these documents are in the archives.

of notes on Balliol history, of which the bulk are derived from these two antiquarians; but he intersperses some reminiscences of his own.

Rawlinson MSS. D. 317, *fol.* 201. Assessment of the various Colleges to the poor-rate.

Wood MSS. F. 28, *fol.* 54. List of Balliol Fellows in the sixteenth century, compiled with some care from the Register.

C.—General Printed Authorities.

Statutes printed for the University Commission of 1852.

Reports of the Commissions of 1852 and 1874.

Register of the University, 1521–71 (Oxford Hist. Soc., ed. Boase).

Register of the University, 1571–21 (Oxford Hist. Soc., ed. Clark).

Gutch, *Collectanea Curiosa,* vol. i.

Burrows' *Register of the Parliamentary Visitation* (Camden Soc.).

Wood's *Athenae, Life and Times, Colleges and Halls, Annals, Fasti.*

Peshall's *History of the University of Oxford.*

Maxwell Lyte, *History of the University of Oxford.*

Foster's *Alumni Oxonienses.*

State Papers, Domestic, 1653–54, 1638–39, 1623–25, 1667–68.

Calendar of Patent Rolls, 1281–92.

Papal Letters and Petitions (State Papers).

Surtees' *History of Durham,* vol. iv., part ii.; vol. i. pp. xl. *ff.*

Little's *Grey Friars in Oxford* (Oxford Hist. Soc.).

Memorie of the Somervilles (ed. Sir W. Scott).

Shirley's *Fasciculi Zizaniorum.*

Lechler's *Wyclif* (tr. Lorrimer).
Poole's *Life of Wyclif*.
Records of the English Province, S.J. vi. p. 679 (ed. Foley).
James' *The Jesuits' Downfall* (1612).
Dunsford's *Tiverton*.
Prince's *Worthies of Devon* (s. v. Blundell).
Laud's *History of his Chancellorship*.
Heylin's *Cyprianus Redivivus*.
Evelyn's *Diary and Correspondence*.
Letters of Humphrey Prideaux (Camden Soc.).
Christie's *Life of Shaftesbury*.
Bliss, *Reliquiae Hearnianae*.
Diary of Thomas Hearn (Oxford Hist. Soc.).
Blacow, *Letter to W. King, LL.D.* (London, 1755).
Terrae Filius (Oxford, 1733).
G. Birkbeck Hill's *Johnson and his Critics*.
Nichols' *Literary History of Eighteenth Century*.
    ,,   *Anecdotes*.
Rae's *Life of Adam Smith*.
Smith's *Wealth of Nations*, part v. chap. i.
Life and Letters of Southey (by C. Southey).
Veitch's *Life of Sir W. Hamilton*.
Hamilton's *Discussions*, p. 750, fol.
Prothero's *Life and Letters of Dean Stanley*.
Ward's *W. G. Ward and the Oxford Movement*.
Davidson and Benham, *Life of Abp. Tait*.
Campbell and Abbot, *Life of B. Jowett*.
    ,,   ,,   ,,   *Letters of B. Jowett*.
F. Oakeley, in *The Month*, vol. iv. p. 50.
Andrew Lang, *Life of Lord Iddesleigh*.
W. Knight, *Life of J. C. Shairp*.

II.—VISITORS OF THE COLLEGE FROM 1520*

(Based on Dr. Wall's List)

c. 1522. John Langland, Bishop of Lincoln.

1525. The election of W. Whyte to the Mastership is confirmed by Dr. Aleyn, Commissary-General for the Visitations of the most reverend Father, Thomas, by divine mercy of the title of St. Cecilia (Wolsey).

c. 1531. Richard Stubbs.

c. 1539. Thomas Cromwell (in his capacity of Vicar-General).

c. 1553. John Whyte, Bishop of Lincoln.
c. 1557. Thos. Watson, ,, ,,
c. 1559. Nicholas Bullingham, ,, ,,
c. 1570. Thos. Cowper, ,, ,,
c. 1585. William Wickham, ,, ,,
c. 1595. William Chadderton, ,, ,,
c. 1609. William Barlow, ,, ,,
c. 1613. Richard Neile, ,, ,,

1617-37. No record.

c. 1637. William Laud. First mentioned in connection with the election of Thos. Lawrence to the Mastership.

1642. Thomas Winaffe, Bishop of Lincoln.

1663. Benjamin Laney, ,, ,,

[Bishop Fuller of Lincoln, said by Stinton to have acted as Visitor.]

1675. Thos. Barlow, Bishop of Lincoln. Elected while Provost.

1691. Dr. Busby of Queen's. First instance of free election.

* In the seventeenth century only the dates when the Visitors are first mentioned can be given. No record of their installation is preserved.

1694. Henry Compton, Bishop of London.
1723. Dr. Brydges, Canon of Rochester, Rector of Amersham.
1728. Sir John Dolben, D.D., Canon of Durham.
1755. Sir William Bunbury.
1763. Robert Drummond, Abp. of York.
1777. Frederick Cornwallis, Abp. of Canterbury.
1781. John Moore, Abp. of Canterbury.
1806. Shute Barrington, Bp. of Durham.
1827. William Howley, Bp. of London.
1848. John Kaye, Bp. of Lincoln.
1854. John Jackson, Bp. of Lincoln.
1885. Lord Bowen.
1894. Viscount Peel.

III.—THE BOAT CLUB

A.—Blues since 1864.

1864. W. Awdrey.
1865. A. Morrison.*
1868. W. D. Benson. S. D. Darbishire.
1869. W. D. Benson. S. D. Darbishire.
1870. W. D. Benson. S. D. Darbishire. J. Edwards. Moss.
1871. J. Edwards Moss.
1877. W. H. Grenfell. T. G. Mulholland.
1878. W. H. Grenfell.
1898. F. W. Warre. A. T. Herbert.
1899. F. W. Warre. A. T. Herbert. E. L. Warre. C. W. Tomkinson. A. D. Steel.

B.—Crews which have rowed at the head of the river.

1873. (Went Head.)

Bow, A. L. Smith.
2, A. F. Acland Hood.
3, R. H. Roe.
4, H. G. Wedderburn.

* The cup for the Morrison Fours was not presented to the Club by this gentleman, but by Mr. G. Morrison in the year 1860. The crew by whom the Fours were won in that year was made up as follows:

Bow, G. Brander.
2, J. Tomkinson.
3, Viscount Duncan.
Stroke, G. F. Mylne.
Cox., J. R. Langford.

5, A. W. Mulholland.
6, S. D. Darbishire.
7, F. E. H. Elliot.
Stroke, W. Farrar.
Cox., R. J. Knowling.

1874. (Two nights.)

Bow, A. L. Smith.
2, G. H. Armitstead.
3, R. H. Roe.
4, D. B. Wilson.
5, A. F. Acland Hood.
6, F. J. N. Pearson.
7, P. J. Hornby.
Stroke, A. W. Mulholland.
Cox., J. J. Massingham.

1879. (Went Head.)

Bow, W. H. P. Rowe.
2, E. A. Upcott.
3, J. Twigg.
4, M. R. Portal.
5, H. C. Lowther.
6, A. A. Wickens.
7, S. B. Crossley.
Stroke, W. A. B. Musgrave.
Cox., B. W. Randolph.

In 1880 the Eight went down on the first night.

C.—The First Torpid went Head for the first time in 1897, and maintained that position in 1898 and 1899.

INDEX

ABBOLDESLEY, or Abbotsley, 29-30, 31
Abbott, George, Abp., 90, 98, 107, 115, 116, 125, 126, 127
Abbott, Robert, 112, 113, 116, 117
Abdy, Robert, 41, 47, 52
Abingdon, 126
Act, the, 145
Alexander VI., 65
All Souls College, 3, 89, 145, 167
Angelus, Christopher, 114, 115
Armada, the, 97
Armagh, Richard of, 23, 25, 26, 28, 39
Arnold, Matthew, 196, 209, 212
Ascham, Robert, 78, 80, 90
Athletics, 206, 222, 231

BABINGTON, Francis, 89, 95, 105
Bacon, Francis Lord, 113
Bacon, Nathaniel and Nicholas, 125
Bagshaw, Christopher, 107-109
Balliofergus, v. *Savage*, Henry
Balliol Hall, Old, 9, 14, 15, 18, 104
Balliol Hall, New, 15
Balliol, Dervorguilla de, 10, 11, 17; her statutes, 12, 13, 14, 24, 25, 26, 32, 66
Balliol, Edward, 11, 17, 31
Balliol, John, 7, 8, 16, 36
Baron, Dr., 168, 169, 178

Baskerville, Hannibal, 144, 151, 152, 154, 226
Batellers, the, 152
Bathurst, Dr., 150, 163
"Bayly Hall," 11
Belial, men of, 187
Bell, Alexander, 50
Bell, William (1496), 41, 47
Bell, William (1564), 111
Bere Regis, Dorset, 166, 171
Berners, Lord, 53
Best, Mr., 179 ff., 183
Blacow, Canon, 185 ff.
Blagdon Exhibition, 166
Blundell, Peter, 121-2. His foundation, 122 ff., 162, 165, 167, 177
Brackenburg, Miss, 220
Bradshaw, George, 127, 129, 135, 138
Bridgman, Sir Orlando, 158
Bristol, City of, 164. Buildings, *ib.*
Brookes, James, 76, 86-88
Brydges, Dr., 169, 180-182
Burnel, William, 19, 160
Bury, Richard, 27-8, 30
Busby, Dr., 151, 162, 164
Bushell, Thomas, 119
Butterfield, Mr., 214

CÆSAR'S Lodgings, 126
Calstone, Wilts, 166

INDEX

Campian, Father, 109
Canterbury Hall, 39, 40, 160
Capgrave, 51
Carlisle, Bp. of, 65, 66
Catharine, St. of Alexandria, 9 n., 15 (v. Chapel).
Catharine Wheel, the, 104
Chace, Thomas, 41, 47
Chapel, the 1st, 26, the 2nd, 27, the 3rd, 77-80, the New, 214
Charles I., 118, 130, 131, 132, 133, 134
Cheynell, Francis, 130, 138
Chicheley, Abp., 42
Chimers Hall, 18, 160
Chirkham, Walter, 7, 8
Christ Church College, 90, 112, 149, 152
Chrysoloras, 48
Church Handborough, Oxfordshire, 101
Clabrook, John, 121
Claymond, Dr., 66
Clayton, Thomas, 113
Clifford, Richard, 47 n.
Clough, A. H., 208, 209, 210
Coleridge, S. T., 199, 200
Compton, Henry, 164, 166
Conopius, Nathaniel, 115
Cootes, George, 76, 82-87
Cornubia, Stephen de, 26
Crabtree, Mr., 127
Cranmer, Abp., 87, 88
Coventry, Sir Thomas, 99
Coventry, Thomas Lord, 99
Critopylus, Metrophanes, 115
Cromwell, Thomas, 82-85
Crouch, Nicholas, 140, 166
Cruwys, William, 177

Danvers, Lady Anna, 82
Davenport, Sir Humphrey, 99
Davey, Dr., 168, 201

Dawes, Mr., 186
Derby, Robert, 22, 38
Dervorguilla, v. *Balliol*, Dervorguilla de
Despenser, Hugh le, 19
Docton, Mr., 171
Dolben, Sir John, 169, 183
Ducket, Mr., 166
Dunch Exhibition, 121, 155, 175
Durham, Bps. of, 7, 8, 27-8, 30, 32 (v. *Bury*, *Chirkham*.)
Durham College, 2, 26, 28, 32, 44

Edmund's Hall, St., 90, 115
Edward IV., 56, 57
Ellis, Edmund, 140, 141
Emanuel College, 122, 123
Eveleigh, Dr., 202
Evelyn, John, 114, 115, 127, 128, 164, 165
Exeter College, 22, 96, 110, 113

Fanshawe, Mrs., 132
Farely, Elias, 129
Farmer, Mr., 221
Feckyngton, John, 63
Felton Foundation, the, 28-31
Fielden, Mr., 184
Fillingham, 37, 38
Fisher's Buildings, 170, 171, 198
Fisher, Mr. Henry, 177
Fotheringhay, *Walter of*, q.v.
Foster, Antony, 111
Fox's Statutes, 12, 55, 58, 65, 66 ff., 90, 95, 103, 177, 181
Franciscans, the, 5, 6, 12, 16 (v. *Procuratores*)

Garnett, Antony, 91, 95
Garnett, Thomas, 106
Gloucester Hall, 3, 156
Goode, John, 141

INDEX

Goode, Dr. Thomas, 148, 150, 151, 156, 164, 165, 166
Gotham, William de, 27
Grace, the College, 147
Gray, Bp. of Ely, 47, 50 ff., 89
Greaves, John, 120
Green, T. H., 217, 218, 219
Guarino da Verona, 48, 49, 50, 51, 53, 54
Gunthorpe, John, 54, 55

HAMILTON, Sir William, 157, 159, 173, 188, 189
Hammond's Lodgings, 103, 104
d'Harcourt, Collège, 3
Hartlepool, Hugh of, 12
Hearne, Thomas, 143, 168, 170
Heberden, Mr., 221
Henrietta Maria, 119
Henry III., 8, 9
Henry VI., 56
Henry VII., 55
Henry VIII., 80, 81, 84
Hertford College, 159
Hert Hall, 18, 19
Holland, Thomas, 96, 110, 113, 116
Hôtel Dieu, 2
Howell, Thomas, 153 ff.
Hugate, John, 22, 28
Hugh le *Despenser*, *q.v.*
Hugh's Hall, St., 18
Hugh de *Vienne*, *q.v.*
Humphrey, Duke, 53
Hunt, Dr., 168, 170
Huntspill, Somerset, 171
Hutchins, Mr., 171

ISLIP, Simon, 39, 40

JENKYNS, Dr., 159, 189, 193, 202 ff., 209, 213, 214
Jesus College, Oxford, 113
Jewel, Bp., 87

Jowett, Benjamin, 126, 145, 193 210 ff., as Master 214 ff.
Julius II., 65

KEMP, Bp., 63
Kemyss, Lawrence, 97
Kettell, Dr., 131, 132
Kyrle, John, 142 ff.

LATIMER, Bp., 87, 88
Laud, Abp., 74, 114, 116, 117, 118, 128, 130, 132
Lawrence St., Jewry, London, 19 n., 20
Lawrence, Dr. Thomas, 112, 113, 120, 127, 128, 131–133, 136, 138
Layton, 81
Lechler, Life of Wyclif, 33, 40
Leicester, Earl of, 105
Leigh, Dr. Theophilus, 168, 179, 181, 183, 184, 186
Lilly, Edmund, 95, 109, 116, 117
Lincoln, Bps. of, 17, 73, 74, 83, 84, 130
Lincoln College, 90, 105, 113, 136
Littlecote, 100
Locke, John, 162
London, Bps. of, 33, 47 n., 62, 63, 73, 164, 166
London, Fire of, 162, 165
London, Dr., 81
Lux, Mr., 181
Luxmore, Mr., 186
Lyte, Maxwell, Mr., 225

MADAN, Mr., 226
Magdalen College, 112, 113, 131, 132, 145
Mander, Dr. Roger, 148, 164, 166
Manning, Cardinal, 206
Mark's Tey, Essex, 171
Martyrs' Memorial, 88
Mary Magdalen, St., 16
Mary, Queen, 92

INDEX

Mayfield, 39
Menyl, William de, 12
Merry, Mr., 186
Merton College, 3, 10, 23, 39, 113, 131, 145, 149
Mickle Benton, 30, 31
Monmouth, Duke of, 163
Monson, Edmund, 98
Moore, Ferryman, 127
More, Sir Thomas, 53, 59
Morrison Fours, the, 231
Morton, John, Cardinal, 55-58

NETTLESHIP, R. L., 198, 219
Neville, George, 27, 55, 56, 60
New College, 3, 22, 112, 131
Newman, Mr. W. L.,
Newte Exhibition, 172, 175

OAKELEY, Frederick, 207, 208
Ogilvie, Mr., 205
Oriel College, 22, 90

PADUA, Univ. of, 48, 108
Palmer, Archdeacon, 212
Paravicini, Baroness de, 16, 84, 224
Parker, W. J., 225
Parkhurst, John, 112, 117, 120, 129
Parkinson, Mr., 186
Parsons, Bp., 168, 176, 184, 188, 193, 201, 202
Parsons, Robert, 89, 106 ff.
Pembroke College, 113, 117, 126
Periham, Lady Elizabeth, 121, 125-6
Philobiblon, 28
Piers, John, 95, 109
Poleter, Adam, 27
Poole, Mr. R. L., 7, 75, 224
Poore, Mr., 137
Pope, Alexander, 143, 144
Popham, Sir John, 99 f., 122-124
Powell, Mr., 173

Prideaux (quoted), 150
Procuratores, the, 12, 13, 14, 21, 24-7, 32, 33, 62, 63, 64, 66

QUAPPELAD, Nicholas, 27
Queen's College, Oxford, 22, 23, 44, 111, 115
Quick, Mr., 181

RALEIGH, Sir Walter, 98, 100
Rashdall, Mr., 225
Ratcliffe, Dr., 164
Reading, Abbot of, 27
Richard of *Armagh*, q.v.
Riddell, J., 212
Riley, Mr. T. H., 225
Robinson, Bp., 171, 178, 226
Robsart, Amy, 105, 111
Roderham, Richard, 63
Rogers, the Rev. W., 204

SANFORD, Mr., 178
Savage, Dr. Henry, 9 n., 115, 120, 128, 138, 139, 142, 148, 160, 161, 164, 224
Savage, Mrs., 140
Scott, Dr., 193, 213, 214, 221
School Street, 18, 19
Shaftesbury, Lord, 158, 162, 163
Sidney Sussex College, 122, 123
Singe, George, 120
Slikebarne, Richard, 16
Smith, Adam, 172, 173, 191
Smith, Henry, 212
Snell, John, his foundation, 155, 157, 183
Somervyle, Sir Philip, his foundation, 30 ff., 34 ff., 62
Sorbonne, 3
Southey, Robert, 174, 187, 188, 190, 199
Split Crow, the, 150
Spurway, Mr., 137

INDEX

Squib, Auditor, 161
Squier, Adam, 90, 95, 107
Stamfordham, 15, 130, 170
Stapylton, Robert, 41, 49
Stinton, Dr. (quoted), 178
Stubbs, Lawrence, 79, 80
Stubbs, Richard, 76, 77
Sudbury, Simon, 33, 62, 64
Sutton, Bp., 17
Synagogue, the, 19

TAIT, Abp., 159, 205, 208, 209, 210
Terrae Filius, the, 187, 192; the Balliol, 145
Tetbury, 172
Thickness or Thickens, Jas., 127, 137, 145
Thorne, Giles, 118
Thwaytes, Robert, 41, 47, 50, 55
Thynne, Lady Isabella, 132
Tiptoft, Lord, 53
Tisdale, Thomas, 126
Tonson, Jacob, 144
Toynbee, Arnold, 217-18
Trinity College, Oxford, 131
Trymnall, Bp., 166

UNIVERSITY College, 90, 113
Urban V., 32, 33

VENN, John, 148, 163, 164
Vienne, Hugh de, 20
Visitors, the, of Balliol, 73, 105, 128, 130, 135 ff., 151, 162, 164, 166, 169, 171, 175, 180 ff., 214, 229

Visitors (contd.)—(v. *Laud, Busby, Brydges, Dolben, Compton, Winstaffe*; also *Appendix I.*)
Vittorino da Felbre, 49, 50

WADHAM, Nicholas, 79
Wall, Dr., 226
Walker of Fotheringhay, 16, 17
Ward, W. G., 207-9
Warkenby, Hugh of, 27
Warner foundation, the, 155-7, 162, 226
Warner, Dr. John, 111
Waterhouse, Mr., 220
Watson, Joshua, 202
Wendy, Sir Thomas, 166
Wenman, Dr., 113
Wentworth, Peter, 79, 120
White, Mr., 153 ff.
Whitefield, George, 153
Whitmore, Mr., 186
Whyte, William, 76, 82, 83
Wichnor, Staffordshire, 30, 34
Wight, the Rev. Mr., 172
Wightwick, Richard, 126
Winstaffe, Bp., 130
Wodeford, Friar, 40
Wolsey, Cardinal, 81
Wood, Anthony, 46, 52, 53, 55, 78, 87, 91, 107, 134, 145, 244
Woollcombe, Mr., 205
"Worcester College," Balliol known as, 165
Wryght, William, 76, 85, 86, 87, 89
Wyatt, Mr., 190, 200
Wyclif, John, 23, 30, 37 *ff.*, 42

TIMES.—"We are glad to welcome the first two volumes of what promises to be an excellent series of College Histories... Well printed, handy and convenient in form, and bound in the dark or light blue of either University, these small volumes have everything external in their favour. As to their matter, all are to be entrusted to competent men, who, if they follow in the steps of the first two writers, will produce records full of interest to everybody who cares for our old Universities."

Universities of Oxford and Cambridge

Two Series of Popular Histories of the Colleges

To be completed in Twenty-one and Eighteen Volumes respectively

EACH volume will be written by some one officially connected with the College of which it treats, or at least by some member of that College who is specially qualified for the task. It will contain: (1) A History of the College from its Foundation; (2) An Account and History of its Buildings; (3) Notices of the Connection of the College with any important Social or Religious Events; (4) A List of the Chief Benefactions made to the College; (5) Some Particulars of the Contents of the College Library; (6) An Account of the College Plate, Windows, and other Accessories; (7) A Chapter upon the best known, and other notable but less well-known Members of the College.

Each volume will be produced in crown octavo, in a good clear type, and will contain from 200 to 250 pages (except two or three volumes, which will be thicker). The illustrations will consist of full-page plates, containing reproductions of old views of the Colleges and modern views of the buildings, grounds, &c.

The two Series will extend over a period of about two years, and no particular order will be observed in the publication of the volumes. The writers' names are given on the next page.

Price 5s. net per Volume

These volumes can be ordered through any bookseller, or they will be sent by the Publishers on receipt of published price together with postage.

Oxford Series

COLLEGES	
University	A. C. Hamilton, M.A.
Balliol	H. W. Carless Davis, M.A.
Merton	B. W. Henderson, M.A.
Exeter	W. K. Stride, M.A.
Oriel	D. W. Rannie, M.A.
Queen's	Rev. J. R. Magrath, D.D.
New	Rev. Hastings Rashdall, M.A.
Lincoln	Rev. Andrew Clark, M.A.
All Souls	C. Grant Robertson, M.A.
Magdalen	Rev. H. A. Wilson, M.A.
Brasenose	J. Buchan.
Corpus Christi	Rev. T. Fowler, D.D.
Christ Church	Rev. H. L. Thompson, M.A.
Trinity	Rev. H. E. D. Blakiston, M.A.
St. John's	Rev. W. H. Hutton, B.D.
Jesus	E. G. Hardy, M.A.
Wadham	J. Wells, M.A.
Pembroke	Rev. Douglas Macleane, M.A.
Worcester	Rev. C. H. O. Daniel, M.A.
Hertford	S. G. Hamilton, M.A.
Keble	D. J. Medley, M.A.

Cambridge Series

Peterhouse	Rev. T. A. Walker, LL.D.
Clare	J. R. Wardale, M.A.
Pembroke	W. S. Hadley, M.A.
Caius	J. Venn, Sc.D., F.R.S.
Trinity Hall	H. T. Trevor Jones, M.A.
Corpus Christi	Rev. H. P. Stokes, LL.D.
King's	Rev. A. Austen Leigh, M.A.
Queens'	Rev. J. H. Gray, M.A.
St. Catharine's	The Lord Bishop of Bristol.
Jesus	A. Gray, M.A.
Christ's	J. Peile, Litt.D.
St. John's	J. Bass Mullinger, M.A.
Magdalene	W. A. Gill, M.A.
Trinity	Rev. A. H. F. Boughey, M.A., and J. Willis Clark, M.A.
Emmanuel	E. S. Shuckburgh, M.A.
Sidney	G. M. Edwards, M.A.
Downing	Rev. H. W. Pettit Stevens, M.A., LL.M.
Selwyn	Rev. A. L. Brown, M.A.

www.ingramcontent.com/pod-product-compliance
Lightning Source LLC
Chambersburg PA
CBHW031350230426
43670CB00006B/490